WORLD CRISIS
AND
THE PATHWAY TO PEACE

WORLD CRISIS
AND
THE PATHWAY TO PEACE

A Compilation of Speeches and Letters

of

Ḥaḍrat Mirza Masroor Ahmad

Imam and the Head of the Worldwide Aḥmadiyya Muslim Jamāʿat,
Fifth Successor to the Promised Messiah[as], may Allah the Almighty be his help

ISLAM INTERNATIONAL PUBLICATIONS LTD.

World Crisis and the Pathway to Peace

A Compilation of Speeches and Letters
of
Ḥaḍrat Mirza Masroor Ahmad,
Imam and the Head of the Worldwide Aḥmadiyya Muslim Jamāʿat,
Fifth Successor to the Promised Messiah[as]

First Published in the UK: 2012 [ISBN: 978-1-84880-079-3]
[Third and Fourth Ed. with additions]

**Fifth Edition [with additions] Published in the UK in 2016
Reprinted: India, UK and USA in 2017**

© Islam International Publications Ltd.

Published by
Ahmadiyya Muslim Community, USA
15000 Good Hope Road
Silver Spring, MD 20905 USA
www.trueislam.com
1-800-949-4752 (1-800-Why-Islam)

ISBN (hardback): 978-1-84880-857-7
ISBN (paperback): 978-1-84880-858-4

CONTENTS

About the Author .... *ix*
Foreword .... *xiii*

Speeches

Islamic Perspective on the Global Crisis 3
Islam's Teachings of Loyalty and Love for One's Nation 23
The Devastating Consequences of a Nuclear War and the
Critical Need For Absolute Justice 39
The Path to Peace—Just Relations Between Nations 63
The Key to Peace—Global Unity 93
Can Muslims Integrate Into Western Societies? 115
Islam—A Religion of Peace and Compassion 133
World Peace—The Critical Need of the Time 151
World Peace & Security—The Critical Issues of Our Time 167
The Keys to Peace in a Time of Global Disorder 183

Letters to the World Leaders

Letter to His Holiness Pope Benedict the XVI..........................201

Letter to the Prime Minister of Israel 207

Letter to the President of the Islamic Republic of Iran.............211

Letter to the President of the United States of America...........215

Letter to the Prime Minister of Canada.....................................219

Letter to the Custodian of the Two Holy Places the King
of the Kingdom of Saudi Arabia...223

Letter to the Premier of the State Council of the People's
Republic of China...227

Letter to the Prime Minister of the United Kingdom 233

Letter to the Chancellor of Germany..237

Letter to the President of the French Republic 241

Letter to Her Majesty the Queen of the United Kingdom
and Commonwealth Realms..247

Letter to the Supreme Leader of the Islamic Republic
of Iran 253

Letter to The President of the Russian Federation 257

Publishers' Note...261

Glossary..265

Ḥaḍrat Mirza Masroor Ahmad
Khalīfatul-Masīḥ V[aba]

ABOUT THE AUTHOR

His Holiness, Mirza Masroor Ahmad, Khalīfatul-Masīḥ V[aba], is the supreme head of the worldwide Aḥmadiyya Muslim Community. He is the fifth successor of the Promised Messiah and Reformer, Ḥaḍrat Mirza Ghulam Ahmad[as] of Qadian.

His Holiness was born on September 15, 1950 in Rabwah, Pakistan to the late Mirza Mansoor Ahmad and the late Nāṣirah Begum Ahmad. Upon completing his Masters Degree in Agricultural Economics in 1977 from the Agriculture University in Faisalabad, Pakistan, he formally dedicated his life to the service of Islam. He was sent to Ghana in 1977 where, for several years, he served as a principal of various Aḥmadiyya Muslim schools.

Later when His Holiness returned to Pakistan, he served in various capacities at the Headquarters of the Aḥmadiyya Community in Rabwah. In 1999, His Holiness was imprisoned for a short period of time on the completely false charge or erasing words of the Holy Qur'an from a sign.

Elected to the lifelong position of Khalīfah (Caliph) of the Aḥmadiyya Muslim Community on 22nd April 2003, His Holiness serves as the worldwide spiritual and administrative head of an international religious organization with tens of millions of members spread across more than 200 countries.

Since being elected Khalīfah, His Holiness has led a worldwide campaign to convey the peaceful message of Islam, through all forms of print and digital media. Under his leadership, national branches of the Aḥmadiyya Muslim Community have launched campaigns that reflect the true and peaceful teachings of Islam. Ahmadi Muslims the world over are engaged in grassroots efforts to distribute millions of 'Peace' leaflets to Muslims and non-Muslims alike, host interfaith and peace symposia and present exhibitions of the Holy Qur'an to present its true and noble message. These campaigns have received worldwide media coverage and demonstrate that Islam champions peace, loyalty to one's country of residence and service to humanity.

In 2004, His Holiness launched the annual National Peace Symposium in which guests from all walks of life come together to exchange ideas on the promotion of peace and harmony. Each year, the symposium attracts many serving ministers, parliamentarians, politicians, religious leaders and other dignitaries.

His Holiness has travelled globally to promote and facilitate service to humanity. Under the leadership of His Holiness, the Aḥmadiyya Muslim Community has built a number of schools and hospitals that provide excellent education and healthcare facilities in remote parts of the world.

His Holiness strives to establish peace at every level of society. He constantly advises members of the Aḥmadiyya Muslim

Community to carry out a 'Jihad' (or struggle) of the self to strive to reform individually, which is the true and biggest form of 'Jihad,' so that every Ahmadi Muslim can establish peace on an individual level first of all, and then be enabled to help others also find peace.

His Holiness gives the same message to all others. In response to a question relating to peacebuilding by a non-Muslim guest at a special reception in Melbourne, His Holiness said: "If you have peace in you, it means that you are projecting peace. And if every one of us had peace, it means that we would be projecting peace to others."

At an individual and collective level, on local, national and international platforms, His Holiness is striving to advise all others of the practical means of establishing peace, based on the true teachings of Islam.

His Holiness, Mirza Masroor Ahmad[aba] currently resides in London, England. As spiritual leader of Ahmadi Muslims all over the world, he vigorously champions the cause of Islam through a refreshing message of peace and compassion.

FOREWORD

The world is passing through very turbulent times. The global economic crisis continues to manifest newer and graver dangers almost every week. The similarities to the period just before the Second World War continue to be cited and it seems clear that events are moving the world at an unprecedented pace towards a horrific third world war. There is an overwhelming sense that things are quickly getting out of control and the people are looking for someone to step on to the stage to offer concrete and solid guidance in which they can have confidence and that speaks to their heart and mind alike and gives them hope that there is a path that can lead to peace. The consequences of a nuclear war are so catastrophic that none dare even think about them.

Here, in this book, we have gathered the guidance put forth by Ḥaḍrat Mirza Masroor Ahmad, the Head of the worldwide Ahmadiyya Muslim Community. Over the past several years, as events have unfolded, he has been fearless in announcing to the

world where things are heading—not to create alarm but to prepare them to think about how the world has arrived in this state
of being and how it can avert disaster and chart a course to peace
and security for all the people that inhabit this global village. He
has forthrightly proclaimed that the only way to insure peace is
for the world to adopt the ways of humility and justice and to
humbly, submissively, turn to God; for man to become humane;
for the strong to treat the weak with dignity and respect and
justice and for the weak and poor to also to show gratitude and
adopt the ways of truth and righteousness and for all to turn to
their Creator in utter humility and total sincerity.

Again and again he has reminded one and all that the way
back from the brink of disaster is for nations to make justice an
absolute requirement of their dealings with each other. Even if
there is enmity between them they need to still observe justice
because history has taught us that this is the only way to eliminate
all traces of future hatreds and thus build a lasting peace.

His Holiness has travelled widely to address in person the
people in charge of running the world's greatest nations including historic addresses at the Capitol Hill in Washington
D.C., Houses of Parliament in London, Military Headquarters,
Germany, European Parliament Brussels and New Zealand
National Parliament. These events were attended by leading congressmen, members of parliament, ambassadors, NGO leaders,
religious leaders, professors, policy advisors and journalists. His
Holiness clearly said to them that the requirements of justice are
only fulfilled when all parties and all people are treated equally
and warned of a spiralling world crisis that is the natural outcome

of unjust and inhumane financial and political policies that cease-
lessly escalate tensions between peoples of the world.

This is the teaching of the Holy Qur'an that he has empha-
sized in his letters to the leaders of the world:

**And let not the enmity of a people, that they hindered
you from the Sacred Mosque, incite you to transgress.
And help one another in righteousness and piety; but
help not one another in sin and transgression. And fear
Allah; surely, Allah is severe in punishment. (ch. 5: v. 3)**

To President Obama, he stated:

As we are all aware, the main causes that led to the Second
World War were the failure of League of Nations and the
economic crisis, which began in 1932. Today, leading economists state that there are numerous parallels between the
current economic crisis and that of 1932. We observe that
political and economic problems have once again led to
wars between smaller nations, and to internal discord and
discontentment becoming rife within these countries. This
will ultimately result in certain powers emerging to the
helm of government, who will lead us to a world war. If in
the smaller countries conflicts cannot be resolved through
politics or diplomacy, it will lead to new blocs and groupings to form in the world. This will be the precursor for
the outbreak of a Third World War. Hence, I believe that
now, rather than focusing on the *progress* of the world, it
is more important and indeed essential, that we urgently

increase our efforts to save the world from this destruction. There is an urgent need for mankind to recognise its One God, Who is our Creator, as this is the only guarantor for the survival of humanity; otherwise, the world will continue to rapidly head towards self-destruction.

To President Putin, he wrote:

The present day escalating situation in Syria has prompted me to write to you and commend your effort in bringing the world together onto a table of dialogue rather than the battlefield. An attack would risk a war not only in the region but could have led to a world war. I was therefore very pleased to read your recent article in a major Western newspaper in which you highlighted that such a course of action was extremely dangerous and could lead to the war spreading. Due to your stand, the major powers have refrained and have adopted a more conciliatory stance, agreeing to resolve this issue through diplomatic channels. Certainly, I believe that this has saved the world from a colossal and huge destruction. I particularly agreed with your point that if countries decided to act independently and made unilateral decisions then the United Nations would suffer the same fate as the League of Nations and would fail.

The crisis in Syria and Iran cooled considerably in the latter half of 2013. The British Parliament voted against military intervention in Syria; Russia and the United States agreed on a plan to deal with Syria's chemical weapons; the US avoided launching attacks on Syria and a mutually acceptable nuclear accord with Iran was also settled upon by the major world powers. All welcome developments and in the direction in which His Holiness had been urging the world, but we are still far from being safe and a lasting solution for global peace will require much more work.

It is our sincere prayer that the guidance collected herein may prove a source of guidance for mankind in this time of great danger so that by acting on the principles of justice and humility and by turning to God, man may be blessed with a lasting peace! (*Āmīn*).

The Publisher

SPEECHES

ISLAMIC PERSPECTIVE
ON THE GLOBAL CRISIS

THE BRITISH PARLIAMENT, THE HOUSE OF COMMONS
LONDON, UK, 2008

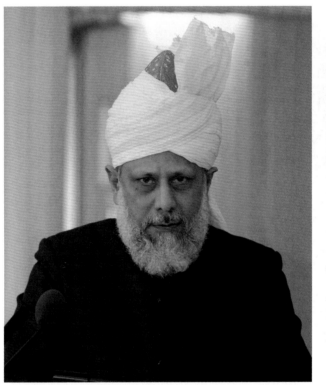

Ḥaḍrat Mirza Masroor Ahmad, Khalīfatul-Masīḥ V[aba] delivering
the keynote address at the House of Commons

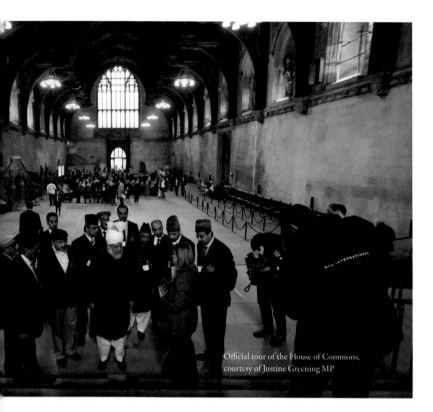

Official tour of the House of Commons,
courtesy of Justine Greening MP

d: Lord Avebury (Liberal Democrats Spokesman for Foreign Affairs), Rt. Hon. Hazel Blears MP (Secretary of State
ommunities and Local Government); Ḥaḍrat Mirza Masroor Ahmad, Khalīfatul-Masīḥ V^aba; Justine Greening MP
ow Treasury Minister); Gillian Merron MP (Foreign Office Minister); Councillor Louise Hyams (the Lord Mayor of
minster). Standing: Jeremy Hunt MP (Shadow Culture Minister); Rafiq Hayat (National Amir AMA UK); Virendra
Marris MP, Rt. Hon. Malcolm Wicks MP (Former Minister at Department for Business, Enterprise and Regulatory Reform);
Marris MP, Simon Hughes MP (President of the Liberal Democrats Party); Martin Linton MP; Alan Keen MP.

Preface

Historic Address by Ḥaḍrat Mirza Masroor Ahmad[aba], Khalīfatul-Masīḥ V, Head of the worldwide Ahmadiyya Muslim Community at the House of Commons (British Parliament) on 22 October 2008.

The reception was organised by Justine Greening, MP for Putney, home to the Fazl Mosque, the Headquarters of the Ahmadiyya Muslim Community, in honour of the completion of 100 years of *Khilāfat-e-Aḥmadiyya*.

In attendance at the reception were Gillian Merron MP, Rt. Hon. Hazel Blears MP, Alan Keen MP, Dominic Grieve MP, Simon Hughes MP, Lord Eric Avebury and also distinguished members of the press, politicians and professionals.

Islamic Perspective on the Global Crisis

Bismillāhir-Raḥmānir-Raḥīm—In the Name of Allah, the Gracious, Ever Merciful.

First of all I would like to thank all of the respected and honourable guests, MPs and Right Honourables who have allowed a leader of a religious organisation to say a few words to you. I am most grateful to our respected MP, Justine Greening, Member of Parliament of our area, who has done so much in organising this event for the sake of a small community of her constituency on the occasion of its Khilāfat Centenary. That shows her greatness, open heartedness and the concern about the sentiments of every people and community living in her constituency.

Although the Ahmadiyya Muslim Community is a small community, it is a standard-bearer and the representative of the true teachings of Islam. Nevertheless, I must say that every Ahmadi who lives in Great Britain is an extremely loyal citizen of the country and loves it; and this is because of the teachings of our Prophet[sa] who instructed us that the love of one's country is an integral part of one's faith.* The teaching of Islam has been further elaborated and emphasised by the Founder of the Ahmadiyya Community, whom we believe to be the Promised Messiah[as] and the Reformer of this Age.

He said that by announcing his claim God Almighty has placed two burdens upon him. One is the right of God and the other is right of God's creation. He went on to say that discharging the rights owed to God's creation was the most difficult and delicate challenge.**

With reference to Khilāfat, you may fear that a time might come when history repeats itself and wars may start as a result of this form of leadership. Let me assure you, however, that although this accusation is laid against Islam, God Willing, the Ahmadiyya Khilāfat will always be known as the standard-bearer of peace and harmony in the world, as well as be loyal to the country in which members reside. The Ahmadiyya Khilāfat is also here to perpetuate and continue the mission of the Messiah and Mahdi, and so there is absolutely no reason to fear the Khilāfat. This Khilāfat draws the attention of members of the Community towards fulfilling these two obligations for which the Promised Messiah[as] came, and as a result, tries to create peace and harmony in the world.

Now, because of the time constraint, I come to the subject matter. If we survey the last few centuries impartially, we will

---

*   *Tafsīr-e-Ḥaqqī, Sūrah al-Qaṣaṣ*, no. 86, and *Fatḥul-Bārī fī Sharḥ Ṣaḥīḥ al-Bukhārī*, Bābo Qaulillāhe Taʿālā Waʾtul-boyūta... and *Tohfatul-Aḥwadhī Sharḥo Jāmiʿ itʾTirmadhī*, Bābo Mā Yaqūl

** *Malfūẓāt*, vol.1, p.326

notice that the wars over that period were not really religious wars. They were more geopolitical in nature. Even in today's conflicts and hostilities amongst nations, we notice that they arise from political, territorial and economic interests.

It is my fear that in view of the direction in which things are moving today, the political and economic dynamics of the countries of the world may lead to a world war. It is not only the poorer countries of the world, but also the richer nations that are being affected by this. Therefore, it is the duty of the superpowers to sit down and find a solution to save humanity from the brink of disaster.

Britain is also one of those countries that can and does exert influence in the developed world as well as in developing countries. You can guide the world, if you so desire, by fulfilling the requirement of equity and justice.

If we look at the recent past, Britain ruled over many countries and left behind a high standard of justice and religious freedom, especially in the sub-continent of India and Pakistan. The Ahmadiyya Muslim Community has witnessed this, and the Founder[as] of the Ahmadiyya Community has greatly praised the British Government on its policies of justice and granting of religious freedom. When the Founder[as] of the Ahmadiyya Community congratulated Her Majesty Queen Victoria on her Diamond Jubilee, and conveyed to her the message of Islam, he specially prayed that, in view of the manner in which the British Government discharges the requirements of justice with equity, may God Almighty reward it generously.

So, our history shows that we have always acknowledged this justice whenever displayed by Britain, and we hope that in future too, justice will remain a defining characteristic of the British Government, not only in religious matters, but in all respects, and that you never forget your good qualities of the past.

Today, there is great agitation and restlessness in the world. We are seeing small-scale wars erupting, while in some places, the superpowers are claiming to try and bring about peace. If the requirements of justice are not fulfilled, the conflagration and flames of these local wars can escalate and embroil the whole world. Therefore, it is my humble request to you to save the world from destruction!

Now, I will briefly mention what the teachings of Islam are to bring about peace in the world, or how peace can be established in the world in the light of these teachings. It is my prayer that to create peace in the world those who are being addressed initially, that is to say the Muslims, may be able to act upon them, but it is a duty of all the countries of the world, all the superpowers or governments, to act upon.

In this day and age when the world has literally shrunk to a global village in a way that could not have been imagined previously, we must realise our responsibilities as human beings and should try to pay attention to solving those issues of human rights that can help to establish peace in the world. Clearly, this attempt must be based on fair play and on fulfilling all the requirements of justice.

Amongst the problems of today, one problem has arisen, if not directly, then indirectly, because of religion. Some groups of Muslims use unlawful means and suicide bombers, bombing in the name of religion to kill and harm non-Muslims including soldiers and innocent civilians, and at the same time to brutally kill innocent Muslims and children. This cruel act is totally unacceptable in Islam.

Due to this ghastly behaviour of some Muslims, a totally wrong impression has developed in non-Muslim countries, and as a result, some parts of the society talk openly against Islam, whilst the others, even though do not speak openly, do not carry a good opinion about Islam in their hearts. This has created distrust in the hearts of the people of Western and non-Muslim countries about Muslims, and because of this attitude of a few Muslims, instead of the situation improving, the reaction of non-Muslims is getting worse by the day.

A primary example of this erroneous reaction is the attack on the character of the Holy Prophet[sa] of Islam and on the Holy Qur'an, the Sacred Book of the Muslims. In this regard, the attitude of British politicians, whatever their party, and of intellectuals in Britain, has been different to that shown by the politicians of some other countries, and I thank you for that. What can the benefit be of hurting such sensitivities apart from increasing hatred and dislike? This hatred spurs certain extremist Muslims into committing 'un-Islamic' deeds, which in turn, provides further opportunity to a number of non-Muslims to air their opposition.

However, those who are not extremists and who deeply love the Holy Prophet[sa] of Islam, are terribly hurt by these attacks and, in this, the Ahmadiyya Jamā'at (Community) is at the forefront. Our single most important task is to show the world the perfect character of the Holy Prophet[sa] and the beautiful teachings of Islam. We, who respect and revere all the Prophets (peace be upon them all) and believe all of them to be the Messengers sent by God, cannot say anything disrespectful against any of them;

but we are very saddened when we hear baseless, untrue allegations against our Prophet[sa].

Nowadays, when the world again is getting divided into blocs; extremism is escalating; and the financial and economic situation is worsening, there is an urgent need to end all kinds of hatred and to lay the foundations of peace. This can only be done by respecting all kinds of sentiments of each other. If this is not done properly, honestly and with virtue, it will escalate into uncontrollable circumstances. I appreciate that economically sound Western countries have generously permitted the people of poor or underdeveloped nations to settle in their respective countries, among whom are Muslims as well.

True justice requires that the sentiments and the religious practices of these people should also be honoured. This is the way by which the peace of mind of people can be kept in tact. We should remember that when the peace of mind of a person is disturbed then the peace of mind of the society is also affected.

As I said earlier, I am grateful to the British legislators and politicians for fulfilling the requirements of justice and for not interfering in this way. This, in fact, is the teaching of Islam that is given to us by the Holy Qur'an. The Holy Qur'an declares that:

There should be no compulsion in religion... (ch. 2: v. 257)

This commandment not only counters the accusation that Islam was spread by the sword, but also tells Muslims that acceptance of faith is a matter between man and his God, and you should not interfere in this in any way. Everyone is permitted to live according to his faith and to perform his religious rituals. However, if there are any practices performed in the name of religion that harm others and go against the law of the land, then the law enforcers of that State can come into action, because if there is any cruel ritual being practised in any religion, it cannot be the teaching of any Prophet of God.

This is the fundamental principle for establishing peace at the local level as well as the international level.

Moreover, Islam teaches us that if as a result of your change of faith, any society, or group or a government tries to interfere in the observance of your religious practice, and thereafter the circumstances change in your favour, then always remember that you must carry no malice or ill-will. You should not think of taking revenge but should rather establish justice and equity. The Holy Qur'an says:

> **O ye who believe! Be steadfast in the cause of Allah, bearing witness in equity; and let not a people's enmity incite you to act otherwise than with justice. Be *always* just, that is nearer to righteousness. And fear Allah. Surely Allah is aware of what you do.** (ch. 5: v. 9)

This is the teaching for peace in society. Never depart from justice even for your enemy. The early history of Islam shows us that this teaching was followed and all the demands of justice were fulfilled. I cannot give too many examples of this but history bears testimony to the fact that after the Victory of Makkah, the Holy Prophet^{sa} did not take any revenge from those who had tormented him but forgave them and allowed them to adhere to their respective faiths. Today, peace can be established only if all requirements of justice are met for the enemy, not only in wars against religious extremists, but also in all other wars. And only such peace is long-lasting.

In the last century, two world wars were fought. Whatever the causes were, if we look deeply, only one cause stands out; and it is that justice was not properly administered in the first instance. As a reaction, what was considered to be an extinguished fire turned out to be cinders that kept on burning slowly, eventually bursting into flames and enveloping the whole world a second time.

Today, restlessness is increasing and wars and actions to maintain peace are becoming the forerunners for another world war. Moreover, the present economic and social problems will be the source of aggravating the situation.

The Holy Qur'an has given some golden principles for establishing peace in the world. It is an established fact that greed causes enmity to grow. Sometimes it manifests itself in territorial expansion or the seizing of the natural resources or, indeed, in impressing the superiority of some upon others. This leads to cruelty, whether it is at the hands of merciless despots who usurp the rights of people and prove their supremacy in pursuit of their vested interests, or it is at the hands of an invading force. Sometimes, the cries and anguish of the cruelly treated people call out to the outside world.

But be that as it may, we have been taught the following golden principle by the Holy Prophet of Islam[sa], which is: help both the afflicted and the cruel.

The Companions of the Prophet[sa] enquired that whereas they could understand helping the afflicted, how could they help a cruel person? The Prophet[sa] responded by saying, 'By stopping his hand from committing cruelty because his excess in cruelty will make him worthy of God's punishment.'* So, out of mercy, you try to save him. This principle extends beyond the smallest fibres of society to the international level. In this connection, the Holy Qur'an says:

> And if two parties of believers fight *against each other*, make peace between them; then *if after that* one of them transgresses against the other, fight the party that transgresses until it returns to the command of Allah. Then if it returns, make peace between them with equity, and act justly. Verily, Allah loves the just. (ch. 49: v. 10)

Though this teaching is about Muslims, yet by adhering to this principle, the foundation of peace on a worldwide basis can be laid.

In order to maintain peace, it has been explained at the outset that the foremost requirement is justice. And, despite abiding by the principle of justice, if efforts to make peace are unsuccessful, then unite and fight collectively against the party that has transgressed and continue until such a time that the transgressing party is ready to make peace. Once the transgressing party is ready to make peace, the requirement of justice is: do not seek revenge, do not impose restrictions or embargoes. By all means, keep an

---

* *Ṣaḥīḥ al-Bukhārī, Kitābul-Ikrāh*, Bābo Yamīnir-Rajule Le Ṣāḥibihī... Hadith no. 6952...

eye on the transgressor but at the same time try and improve his situation.

In order to end the unrest prevalent in some countries of the world today—and unfortunately, some Muslim countries are prominent amongst them—it should be analysed in particular by those nations that have the power to veto, to determine whether or not justice has been properly dispensed. Whenever help is needed, the hands are stretched towards the powerful nations.

As I stated before, we bear testimony to the fact that the history of the British government has always upheld justice and this has encouraged me to draw your attention to some of these matters.

Another principle that we have been taught for restoring peace in the world is not to covetously eye the wealth of others. The Holy Qur'an says:

> **And strain not thy eyes after what We have bestowed on some classes of them to enjoy *for a short time*—the splendour of the present world—that We may try them thereby...** (ch. 20: v. 132)

Greed for any envy of the wealth of others is a cause of increasing restlessness in the world. On a personal basis, keeping up with the Joneses, as the saying goes, has resulted in unending greed and destroyed social peace. Greedy competition on a national basis started and led to the destruction of world peace. This is proven by history and every sensible person can assess that the desire for the wealth of others causes envy and greed to grow and is the source of loss.

This is why God Almighty says that one should keep an eye on one's own resources and derive benefit from them. The effort to make territorial gains is for seeking the benefit of that territory's natural resources. The grouping of nations and the making of power blocs are to procure the natural resources of some countries. In this regard, a number of authors who had previously worked as advisors to the governments have written books detailing how some of the countries endeavour to get control of the resources of other nations. How far the writers are truthful is best known to them, and God knows best, but the situation that emerges from reading these accounts causes serious anguish in the hearts of those who are loyal to their poor countries, and is a major reason for the growth in terrorism and the race for weapons of mass destruction.

Nowadays, the world considers itself more sober, conscious and educated than in the past. Even in the poor countries there are such intelligent souls who have greatly excelled in education in their respective fields. Highly intellectual minds work together in large research centres of the world. Under such circumstances, one should have imagined that people would have joined together and jointly tried to end the wrong ways of thinking and the follies of the past that had resulted in animosities and had led to horrific wars. The God-given intellect and scientific progress should have been used for the betterment of humanity and for devising permissible methods of deriving benefits from one another's resources.

God has bestowed each and every country with natural resources that should have been fully utilised to turn the world into a haven of peace. God has gifted many countries with an excellent climate and environment for growing different crops. Had proper planning been adopted to use modern technology for agriculture, the economy would have strengthened and hunger could have been eliminated from the earth.

Those countries that have been endowed with mineral resources should be allowed to develop and trade at fair prices and openly, and one country should benefit from the resources of the other country. So, this would be the right way, the way that is preferred by God Almighty.

God Almighty sends His messengers to the people so that they can show them the ways that bring people closer to God. At the same time, God says that there is complete freedom in matters of faith. According to our beliefs, reward and punishment will be after death as well. But under the system that God has set up, when the cruelty is inflicted on His creation and justice and fair play are ignored, then by the laws of nature, the after-effects can be seen in this world as well. Severe reactions to such injustice are observed and there can be no guarantee about the reaction being right or wrong.

The true way to conquer the world is that every effort should be made to give the poorer nations their due status.

A major issue today is the economic crisis of what has been termed as the credit crunch. Strange as it may sound, the evidence points towards one fact. The Holy Qur'an guides us by saying: avoid interest because interest is such a curse that it is a danger for domestic, national and international peace. We have been warned that he who accepts interest will one day be as one whom Satan has smitten with insanity. So, we Muslims have been warned that in order to avoid such a situation, stop dealing in interest because money that you get for interest does not enhance your wealth, although on the face of it, it may seem to you that it is increasing. Inevitably, a time comes when its true effects emerge. Furthermore, we have been cautioned that we are not allowed to enter into the business of interest, with the warning that if you do so, it will be a war against God.

This factor is obvious from today's credit crunch. In the beginning there were individuals who borrowed money to buy property; but before they could see ownership of the property they used to die burdened with the debt. But now there are governments that are burdened with debt and smitten as if with insanity. Large companies have become bankrupt. Some banks and financial institutions have folded or been bailed out and this situation prevails in every country, regardless of its being rich or poor. You know better than I do about this crisis. The money of the depositors has been wiped off. Now it depends upon governments as to how and to what extent to protect them. But for the time being, the peace of mind of the families, business-men and leaders of the governments in most countries of the world has all but been destroyed.

Does this situation not compel us to think that the world is heading to the logical conclusion whose warning was given to us well in advance? God knows better what the further consequences of this situation will be.

God Almighty has said: Come towards peace that can only be guaranteed when there is pure and wholesome trade and when resources are put into usage in a proper and fair manner.

Now I end these brief points of our teachings with a reminder that the true peace of the world lies only in turning towards God. May God enable the world to understand this point; only then will they be able to discharge the rights of others.

Finally, I am grateful to all of you again for coming here and listening to me.

Thank you very much.

ISLAM'S TEACHINGS OF LOYALTY
AND LOVE FOR ONE'S NATION

MILITARY HEADQUARTERS
KOBLENZ, GERMANY, 2012

Brigadier General Alois Bach of
the German Federal Army
with Ḥaḍrat Khalīfatul-Masīḥ V[aba]

Ḥaḍrat Khalīfatul-Masīḥ V[aba] addressing
the German Federal Army

1. Colonel Ulrich, 2. Brigadier General Bach, 3. Colonel Trautvetter, and 4. Colonel I.G. Janke, meeting Ḥaḍrat Mirza Masroor Ahmad, Khalīfatul-Masīḥ V[aba]

Islam's Teachings of Loyalty and Love for One's Nation

Bismillāhir-Raḥmānir-Raḥīm—In the Name of Allah, the Gracious, the Merciful.

Assalāmo 'alaikum wa raḥmatullāhe wa barakātohū—peace and blessings of Allah be upon you all.

I would like to first of all take this opportunity to thank all of you for inviting me to your headquarters and giving me the opportunity to say a few words. As the Head of the Ahmadiyya Muslim Community, I would like to speak to you about the teachings of Islam. However, this is such a vast topic, that to cover it in just one function or in a short time is impossible. Thus, it is necessary that I limit myself to one aspect of Islam to focus on and speak to you about.

Whilst contemplating which facet of Islam I should address, I received a request from the National President of our Community here in Germany, Abdullah Wagishauser, in which he asked me to speak about Islam's teachings in relation to love and loyalty to one's nation. This helped me make my decision. Thus, I shall now speak to you briefly about certain aspects of Islam's teachings in this regard.

It is very easy to simply speak of, or hear the words, 'loyalty and love for one's nation.' However, in reality these few words encompass meanings that are wide-ranging, beautiful and of tremendous depth. Indeed, to fully comprehend and understand what these words truly mean and what they require is actually very difficult. In any case, in the short time available, I will try to explain Islam's concept of loyalty and love for one's nation.

First and foremost, a fundamental principle of Islam is that a person's words and deeds should never manifest any form of double standards or hypocrisy. True loyalty requires a relationship built on sincerity and integrity. It requires what a person displays on the surface to be the same as what lies beneath. In terms of nationality, these principles are of the utmost importance. Therefore, it is essential for a citizen of any country to establish a relationship of genuine loyalty and faithfulness to his nation. It does not matter whether he is a born citizen, or whether he gains citizenship later in life, either through immigration or by any other means.

Loyalty is a great quality, and the people who have displayed this attribute to the highest degree and best standards, are the Prophets of God. Their love and bond with God was so strong that in all matters they kept in view His commands and strived to fully implement them, no matter what. This illustrated their commitment to Him and their perfect standards of loyalty. Hence, it is their standards of loyalty that we should use as an example and model. However, before proceeding any further, it is necessary to understand what is actually meant by 'loyalty'.

According to the teachings of Islam, the definition and true meaning of 'loyalty' is the unequivocal fulfilment of one's pledges and covenants at every level and under all circumstances, regardless of difficulty. This is the true standard of faithfulness required by Islam. At various places in the Holy Qur'an, Allah has instructed Muslims that they must fulfil their pledges and covenants, because they will be held to account by Him over all undertakings that they have made. The Muslims have been instructed to fulfil all covenants, including those made with God Almighty, and also all other pledges they have made, according to their respective degrees of importance.

In this context, a question that could arise in the minds of people is that because Muslims claim that God and His religion are of paramount importance to them, thus it follows that their pledge of loyalty to God will be their first priority, and that their covenant to God will be what they value above all else and which they endeavour to fulfil. Therefore, the belief may arise that a Muslim's loyalty to his nation and his pledge to uphold the laws of the land will only be of secondary importance to him. Thus, he may be willing to sacrifice his pledge to his country on certain occasions.

To answer this question, I would firstly like to inform you that the Holy Prophet Muhammad (peace be upon him) himself taught that the 'love for one's nation is a part of faith.' Thus, sincere patriotism is a requirement in Islam. To truly love God and Islam requires a person to love his nation. It is quite clear, therefore, that there can be no conflict of interest between a person's love for

God, and love for his country. As love for one's country has been made a part of Islam, it is quite clear that a Muslim must strive to reach the highest standards of loyalty to his chosen country, because that is a means of reaching God and becoming close to Him. Hence, it is impossible that the love a true Muslim holds for God could ever prove to be an impediment or barrier preventing him from displaying true love and faithfulness towards his country. Unfortunately, we find that in certain countries, religious rights are curtailed or even completely denied. Therefore, another question that can arise is whether those people who are persecuted by their state can still maintain a relationship of love and loyalty to their nation and country. With great sadness, I should inform you that these circumstances exist in Pakistan, where the Government has actually legislated against our Community. These anti-Ahmadiyya laws are practically enforced. Thus in Pakistan, all Ahmadi Muslims have been officially declared by law to be 'non-Muslims'. They are, therefore, forbidden from calling themselves 'Muslim'. The Ahmadis in Pakistan are also prohibited from worshipping in the way Muslims do, or acting in accordance with any Islamic practice or custom that could identify them as a Muslim. Thus, the state itself in Pakistan has deprived members of our Community from their basic human right to worship.

Bearing in mind this state of affairs, it is quite natural to wonder how, in such circumstances, can Ahmadi Muslims follow the laws of the land? How can they continue to display loyalty to the nation? Here I should clarify that where such extreme circumstances exist, then the law, and loyalty to the nation, become two separate issues. We, Ahmadi Muslims, believe that religion is a personal matter for every individual to determine for himself and that there should be no compulsion in matters of faith. Thus, where the law comes to interfere with this right, undoubtedly, it is an act of great cruelty and persecution. Indeed, such state-sanctioned persecution, which has occurred throughout the ages, has been condemned by the vast majority.

If we glance at the history of Europe, we find that people in this Continent have also been the victims of religious persecution, and as a result, many thousands of people had to migrate from one country to the next. All fair-minded historians, governments and people have deemed this to be persecution, and extremely cruel. In such circumstances, Islam advocates that where persecution goes beyond all limits and becomes unbearable, then at that time, a person should leave the town or country and migrate to a place where he is free to practise his religion in peace. However, alongside this guidance, Islam also teaches that under no circumstances should any individual take the law into his own hands and nor should he partake in any schemes or conspiracies against his country. This is an absolutely clear and unequivocal command given by Islam.

Despite the grave persecution they face, millions of Ahmadis continue to live in Pakistan. Despite being subjected to such sustained discrimination and cruelty in all aspects of their lives, they continue to keep a relationship of total loyalty and a true allegiance to the country. Whichever field they work in or wherever they are based, they are constantly engaged in trying to help the nation to progress and succeed. For decades, the opponents of Ahmadiyyat have tried to allege that Ahmadis are not loyal to Pakistan, but they have never been able to prove this or show any evidence to support their claims; instead, the truth is that whenever there has been a need to make any sacrifice for the sake of Pakistan, for the sake of their country, Ahmadi Muslims have always stood at the forefront and been constantly ready to make every sacrifice for the sake of the country.

Despite themselves being a victim and target of the law, it is Ahmadi Muslims who follow and abide by the laws of the land better than anyone else. This is because they are true Muslims, who follow true Islam. Another teaching given by the Holy Qur'an in relation to loyalty is that people should keep away from all things that are immodest, undesirable and that form any type of rebellion. A beautiful and distinguishing feature of Islam is that it does not just draw our attention to the final point of culmination, where the consequences are extremely dangerous; instead, it warns us about all of the smaller issues as well, which act as stepping stones leading mankind to a path paved with danger. Thus, if Islam's guidance is followed properly, then any issue can be resolved at the earliest point, before the situation gets out of hand.

For instance, an issue which can gravely harm a country is financial greed by individuals. Often, people get consumed by material desires that spiral beyond control, and such desires ultimately lead people to act in a disloyal fashion. Thus, such things can ultimately be a cause of treachery against one's country. Let me explain a bit. In Arabic the word *baghā* has been used to describe those people or those acts of people that cause harm to their countries. It refers to those who take part in wrong practices or who inflict harm on others. It also includes those people who commit fraud and so try to acquire things in an illegal or unjust manner. It refers to those people who transgress all limits and so cause harm and damage. Islam teaches that people who act in these ways cannot be expected to act in a loyal manner, because loyalty is intertwined with high moral values. Loyalty cannot exist without high moral values and high moral values cannot exist without loyalty. Whilst it is true that different people may have different views about high moral standards, yet the religion of Islam revolves solely around seeking God's pleasure. Thus, Muslims are instructed to always act in a manner that is pleasing to Him. In short, according to Islamic teachings, God Almighty has forbidden all forms of treachery or rebellion, whether against one's country or one's government. This is because rebellion or acting against the state is a threat to the peace and security of a nation. Indeed, where internal rebellion or opposition occurs, then it fans the flames of external opposition and encourages outsiders to take advantage of the internal disorder. Hence, the consequences of disloyalty to your nation can be far-reaching and extreme. Thus, anything that can cause harm to a nation is included in the term *baghā* that I have described. Keeping all of this in mind, loyalty to one's nation requires a person to display patience, to show morality and to follow the laws of the land.

Generally speaking, in the modern era, most governments are run democratically. Therefore if a person or group wishes to change the government, then they should do so by following the proper democratic process. They should make themselves heard by voting at the ballot box. Votes should not be cast on the basis of personal preferences or personal interests, but in fact, Islam teaches that a person's vote should be exercised with a sense of loyalty and love for his country. A person's vote should be cast with the betterment of the nation in mind. Therefore, a person should not look at his own priorities and from which candidate or party he can personally benefit; instead, a person should make his decision in a balanced way whereby he assesses which candidate or party will help the entire nation progress. The keys to government are a huge trust and thus they should only be handed over to the party who the voter honestly believes is best suited and most deserving. This is the true Islam, and this is true loyalty.

Indeed, in Chapter 4, verse 59 of the Holy Qur'an, Allah has commanded that a person should only hand over trusts to those who are entitled, and that when judging between people, he should make his decision with justice and honesty. Thus, loyalty to one's nation requires that the power of the government should be given to those who are truly entitled to it, so that the nation can progress and come to stand at the forefront amongst the nations of the world.

In many parts of the world we find that members of the public take part in strikes and protests against government policies. Furthermore, in certain Third World countries, the protesters vandalise or damage possessions and properties belonging either to the state or to private citizens. Though they may claim to be acting out of love, the truth is that such acts have nothing to do with loyalty or love for the nation. It should be remembered that even where protests or strikes are conducted peacefully, without recourse to criminal damage or violence, it still can have a very negative effect. This is because even peaceful protests often result in a loss of millions to the economy of the nation. Under no circumstances can such behaviour be considered to be an example of loyalty to the nation. A golden principle taught by the Founder of the Ahmadiyya Muslim Jamā'at was that under all circumstances, we must always remain obedient to Allah, to the Prophets and to the rulers of our nation. This is the same teaching given in the Holy Qur'an. Hence, even where a country permits strikes or protests to take place, they should only be conducted to the extent where they do not harm or cause damage to the nation or to the economy.

Another question that often arises is whether Muslims can join the military forces of the Western countries, and if they are permitted to join, can they then partake in military attacks on Muslim countries? One underlying principle of Islam is that no person should assist in acts of cruelty. This key command must always remain at the forefront of any Muslim's mind. Where a Muslim country is attacked, because it has itself acted in a cruel and unjust manner and took the first step of aggression, then in such circumstances the Qur'an has instructed Muslim governments that they should stop the hand of the oppressor. This means they should stop the cruelty and endeavour to establish peace. Thus, in such circumstances to take action as a means to end cruelty is permissible. However, when the nation which transgresses reforms itself and adopts peace, then that country and its people should not be taken advantage of or be subjugated on the basis of false pretences or excuses. They should instead be granted normal state freedom and independence once again. The military ambition should thus be to establish peace, rather than to fulfil any vested interests.

In the same way, Islam permits all countries, whether Muslim or non-Muslim, the right to stop cruelty and oppression. Thus, if necessary, non-Muslim countries can attack Muslim countries to achieve these genuine aims. Muslims in those non-Muslim countries are allowed to join the armies of those non-Muslim countries and prevent the other country from cruelty. Where such circumstances truly exist then Muslim soldiers, whichever Western army they may be part of, must follow orders and fight if required in order to establish peace. If, however, a military makes a decision to attack another nation unjustly, and thus becomes the oppressor, then a Muslim has the option to leave the army, because then he would be assisting cruelty. By taking this decision it would not mean that he is being disloyal to his country. In fact, in such circumstances, loyalty to his country would demand that he should take such a step and counsel his own government that they should not allow themselves to fall to the same depths as those unjust governments and nations that act in a cruel way. If however, joining the army is compulsory and there is no way to leave, but his conscience is not clear, then the Muslim should leave the country, but cannot raise a voice against the law of the land. He should leave because a Muslim is not permitted to live in a country as a citizen, whilst at the same time, acting against the nation or siding with the opposition.

Thus these are just a few aspects of Islamic teachings, which guide all true Muslims towards the real requirements of loyalty and love for one's country. In the time available I have only been able to briefly touch upon this topic.

Thus in conclusion, I would like to say that today we observe that the world has become a global village. Mankind has become very closely knit together. The people of all nations, religions and cultures are found in all countries. This requires that the leaders of every nation should consider and respect the feelings and sentiments of all people. The leaders and their governments should strive to create laws that foster an environment and spirit of truth and justice, rather than making laws that are a means of causing distress and frustration to the people. Injustices and cruelties should be eliminated and instead we should strive for true justice. The best way to do this is that the world should come to recognise its Creator. Every form of loyalty should be linked to loyalty with God. If this occurs then we will come to witness with our own eyes that the very highest standards of loyalty will be established by the people of all countries and new avenues leading us to peace and security will open throughout the world.

Before ending, I would like to take this opportunity to thank all of you once again for inviting me today and for listening to what I have said. May God bless you all; and may God bless Germany.

Thank you very much.

THE DEVASTATING CONSEQUENCES OF A NUCLEAR WAR AND THE CRITICAL NEED FOR ABSOLUTE JUSTICE

9TH ANNUAL PEACE SYMPOSIUM
LONDON, UNITED KINGDOM, 2012

NATIONAL PEACE SYMPOSIUM
2012

Mayor of London Boris Johnson presenting
His Holiness with a London bus souvenir

Ḥaḍrat Mirza Masroor Ahmad, Khalīfatul-Masīḥ V[aba]
addressing the 9th Annual Peace Symposium

Dame Mary Richardson DBE, UK President
of SOS Children's Villages, accepting
the 'Ahmadiyya Muslim Prize for the
Advancement of Peace' from His Holiness

rat Mirza Masroor Ahmad, Khalīfatul-Masīḥ V[hba]

ng to the overseas Pakistani press regarding world affairs

Preface

On March 24, 2012, the 9th Annual Peace Symposium was held at the Baitul Futūḥ Mosque in Morden—the largest Mosque in Western Europe—organised by the Aḥmadiyya Muslim Jamāʿat (Community) in the UK. The event attracted an audience of more than 1000 people, including government ministers, ambassadors of state, members of both the House of Commons and the House of Lords, the Mayor of London, various other dignitaries, professionals, neighbours and guests from all walks of life. The theme of this year's Symposium was 'International Peace'. The 3rd Annual 'Aḥmadiyya Muslim Prize for the Advancement of Peace' was presented by Ḥaḍrat Mirza Masroor Ahmad[aba] to the charity, 'SOS Children's Villages UK', in recognition of its continued efforts to alleviating the suffering of orphaned and abandoned children around the world and towards fulfilling its vision of 'a loving home for every child.'

Guests in attendance included:

- Rt. Hon. Justine Greening—MP, Secretary of State for Transport
- Jane Ellison—MP (Battersea)
- Seema Malhotra—MP (Feltham and Heston)
- Tom Brake—MP (Carlshalton and Wallington)
- Virendra Sharma—MP (Ealing and Southall)
- Lord Tariq Ahmad—of Wimbledon
- HE Wesley Momo Johnson—the Ambassador of Liberia
- HE Abdullah Al-Radhi—the Ambassador of Yemen
- HE Miguel Solano-Lopez—the Ambassador of Paraguay
- Commodore Martin Atherton—Naval Regional Commander
- Councillor Jane Cooper—the Worshipful Mayor of Wandsworth
- Councillor Milton McKenzie MBE—the Worshipful Mayor of Barking and Dagenham
- Councillor Amrit Mann—the Worshipful Mayor of Hounslow
- Siobhan Benita—independent Mayoral candidate for London
- Diplomats from several other countries including India, Canada, Indonesia and Guinea

The Devastating Consequences
of a Nuclear War and the Critical Need
for Absolute Justice

After reciting *tashahhud, taʻawwudh and bismillāh,* Ḥaḍrat Khalīfatul-Masīḥ V[aba] said:

All our guests—*assalāmo ʻalaikum wa raḥmatullāhe wa barakātohū*—peace and blessings of Allah be upon you all.

Today, after a period of one year, I once again have the opportunity to welcome all of our distinguished guests to this event. I am extremely grateful to all of you, as you have spared your time to come and attend today.

Indeed, most of you are well acquainted with this event which has come to be known as the 'Peace Symposium'. This event is organised each year by the Aḥmadiyya Muslim Community and is just one of our many efforts to try and fulfil our desire for peace to be established in the world.

In attendance today are some new friends, who are attending this function for the first time, whilst others are old friends who have supported our efforts for many years. Regardless, all of you are well-educated and share our desire for peace to be established in the world, and it is due to this desire that you are all attending this event.

All of you are here today with the heartfelt wish that the world comes to be filled with love, affection and friendship. It is this very attitude and these very values that the vast majority of the world longs for and which it stands in need of. In view of all of this, these are the reasons why all of you, who come from different backgrounds, nations and religions, are sitting in front of me today.

As I have said, we hold this conference each year and on each occasion, the same sentiment and hope is expressed by all of us, which is that peace in the world comes to be established before our very eyes; and so each year I also request all of you to endeavour to promote peace wherever you have the opportunity and with whoever you have contact. Furthermore, I also request all those who are linked to political parties or governments that they should also convey this message of peace within their circles of influence. It is essential that everyone is made aware that, for the establishment of world peace, there is a far greater need for high and principled moral values than ever before.

As far as the Aḥmadiyya Community is concerned, wherever and whenever the opportunity arises, we openly express and declare our view that there is only one way to save the world from the destruction and devastation that it is heading towards, and that is that we must all endeavour to spread love, affection and a sense of community. Most importantly, the world must come to recognize its Creator, Who is the One God. This is because it is the recognition of the Creator that leads us towards love and compassion for His Creation, and when this becomes part of our character, it is then that we become recipients of God's Love.

We constantly raise our voice calling for peace in the world, and it is the pain and anguish we feel in our hearts that inspires us to try and alleviate the suffering of mankind and to make the world we live in a better place. Indeed, this very function is just one of our many efforts towards achieving this goal.

As I have already said, all of you also hold these noble desires. Furthermore, I have repeatedly called on politicians and religious leaders to strive for peace. Yet, in spite of all of these efforts, we find that anxiety and turmoil continue to spread and increase throughout the world. In today's world we find so much strife, restlessness and disorder. In some countries members of the public are fighting and waging wars amongst themselves. In some nations the public is fighting against the government, or conversely the rulers are attacking their own people. Terrorist groups are fuelling anarchy and disorder to fulfil their vested interests and so they are arbitrarily killing innocent women, children and the elderly. In some countries, as a means to fulfil their own interests, political parties are warring with each other rather than coming together for the betterment of their nations. We also find some governments and countries are continuously casting their glances enviously in the direction of the resources of other nations. The major powers of the world are consumed by their efforts to maintain their supremacy, and leave no stone unturned in their efforts towards pursuing this goal.

Bearing all of this in mind, we find that neither the Aḥmadiyya

Community nor the majority of you, who are members of the public, have the power or authority to develop policies to bring positive change. This is because we do not hold any governmental power or office. In fact, I would go as far as to say that even the politicians, with whom we have developed friendly relations and who always agree with us when they are in our company, are also unable to speak out. Instead, their voices too are being drowned out and they are prevented from forwarding their views. This is either because they are forced to follow party policies, or perhaps due to external pressures from other world powers or political allies, which are weighing them down.

Nevertheless, we, who take part in this Peace Symposium each year, undoubtedly hold a desire for peace to be established and certainly we express our opinions and feelings that love, compassion and brotherhood should be established amongst all religions, all nationalities, all races and indeed, amongst all people. Unfortunately though, we are powerless to actually bring this vision to light. We do not have the authority or means to achieve the results that we long for.

I recall that a couple of years ago, in this very hall during our Peace Symposium, I delivered a speech detailing the ways and means for world peace to be established, and I also spoke about how the United Nations ought to function. Afterwards, our very dear and respected friend, Lord Eric Avebury, commented that the speech ought to have been delivered at the United Nations itself. Nevertheless, this was a display of his noble character that he was so generous and kind in his remarks. However, what I wish to say is that merely delivering or listening to a speech or lecture is not enough and will not lead to peace being established. In fact, the key requirement to fulfilling this primary goal is absolute justice and fairness in all matters. The Holy Qur'an, in Chapter 4, verse 136, has given us a golden principle and lesson, guiding us about this. It states that as a means to fulfil the requirements of justice, even if you have to bear witness and testify against yourself, your parents or your closest relatives and friends, then you must do so. This is true justice where personal interests are set aside for the common good.

If we think about this principle at a collective level, then we will realise that unfair lobbying techniques based on wealth and influence should be abandoned. Instead, the representatives and ambassadors of each nation should come forward with sincerity and with a desire to support the principles of fairness and equality. We must eliminate all forms of bias and discrimination, as this is the only means to bring about peace. If we look at the United Nations General Assembly or Security Council, we find that often statements or speeches made there receive great praise and acknowledgement, but such tributes are meaningless because the real decisions have already been predetermined.

Thus, where decisions are made on the basis of the pressure or the lobbying of the major powers, as opposed to just and truly democratic means, then such speeches are rendered hollow, meaningless and serve only as pretence to deceive the outside world. Nevertheless, all of this does not mean that we should simply become frustrated, and give up and abandon all our efforts. Instead, it should be our objective, whilst remaining within the laws of the land, to continue to remind the government of the needs of the time. We must also properly advise those groups who have vested interests, so that at a global level, justice can prevail.

Only then will we see the world become the haven of peace and harmony that we all want and desire.

Therefore, we cannot and must not give up our efforts. If we stop raising our voices against cruelty and injustice, then we will become amongst those who have no moral values or standards whatsoever. Whether or not our voices are likely to be heard or have influence is irrelevant. We must continue to counsel others towards peace. I am always extremely pleased when I see that, irrespective of differences of religion or nationality, for the sake of upholding human values, so many people come to this function to listen, to learn and to speak about ways to establish peace and compassion in the world. Thus, I would request all of you to strive for peace to the best of your abilities so that we can keep the flicker of hope alight, that a time will come when true peace and justice will be established in all parts of the world.

We must remember that when human efforts fail, then God Almighty issues His Decree to determine the fate of mankind. Before God's Decree sets into motion and compels people towards Him and towards fulfilling the rights of mankind, it would be far better if the people of the world should themselves come to pay attention to these crucial matters, because when God Almighty is forced to take action, then His Wrath seizes mankind in a truly severe and terrifying manner.

In today's world, one terrifying manifestation of God's Decree could be in the shape of another world war. There is no doubt that the effects of such a war and its destruction will not be limited to the war itself or even to this generation. In fact, its horrific consequences will be exhibited for many generations to come. Just one tragic consequence of such a war will be the effect it will have on new born children, both now and in the future. The weapons available today are so destructive that they could lead to generation after generation of children being born with severe genetic or physical defects.

Japan is the one country to have experienced the abhorrent consequences of atomic warfare, when it was attacked by nuclear bombs during the Second World War. Even today when you visit Japan and meet its people, you see an absolute fear and hatred of war visible in their eyes and from what they say. Yet the nuclear bombs that were used at that time and which caused widespread devastation, were much less powerful than the atomic weapons that are possessed by even very small nations today.

It is said that in Japan, even though seven decades have passed, yet the effects of the atom bombs are still continuing to be manifest on newborn children. If a person is shot by a bullet, then it is sometimes possible for him to survive through medical treatment, but if a nuclear war breaks out, then those who are in the firing line will have no such luck. Instead, we will find that people will instantly die and freeze like statues, and their skin will simply melt away. Drinking water, food and vegetation will all be contaminated and affected by radiation. We can only imagine what type of diseases such contamination will lead to. In those places that are not directly hit and where the effects of the radiation are somewhat less, even there the risk of diseases and illness will become much higher and the future generations will also bear much greater risks.

Therefore, as I have said, the devastating and destructive effects of such warfare will not be limited to the war and its aftermath, but will pass from generation to generation. These are the real consequences of such warfare, and yet today there are selfish and foolish people who are extremely proud of their invention and describe what they have developed as a gift to the world.

The truth is that the so-called beneficial aspects of nuclear energy and technology can be extremely dangerous and lead to widespread destruction, due to either negligence or due to accidents. We have already witnessed such catastrophes, such as the nuclear accident that occurred in 1986 in Chernobyl, in what is now Ukraine, and just last year after the earthquake and tsunami in Japan, it too had to contend with great danger and the country was placed in fear. When such events happen, then it is also very difficult to repopulate the affected regions. Due to their unique and tragic experiences, the Japanese have become extremely cautious and indeed, their sense of fear and terror is fully justified.

It is an obvious statement that people die in wars, and so when Japan entered the Second World War, its Government and its people were well-aware that some people would be killed. It is said that approximately three million people died in Japan, and this came to about 4% of the country's population. Even though a number of other countries may have suffered higher proportions of deaths in terms of total numbers, yet the hatred and aversion to war that we find in the Japanese people remains much higher in comparison to others. The simple reason for this is certainly the two nuclear bombs that were dropped on Japan during World War II, and the consequences of which they are still witnessing and having to bear even today. Japan has proved its greatness and resilience by being able to repopulate and rehabilitate its towns relatively quickly. But let it be clear that if nuclear weapons are used again today, then it is quite possible that parts of certain countries could be completely wiped off the map. They could cease to exist.

Conservative estimates put the death toll of the Second World War at about 62 million and it is said that around 40 million of those who were killed were civilians. Thus, in other words, more civilians died than military personnel. Such devastation occurred despite the fact that apart from in Japan, a traditional war was fought with conventional weapons everywhere else.

The United Kingdom had to bear the loss of around half a million people. Of course, at that time, it was still a colonial power and so its colonies also fought on its behalf. If we include their losses then the death toll rises to millions.

In India alone, around 1.6 million people lost their lives.

However, today the situation has changed, and those very countries that were colonies of the United Kingdom, and who fought for the British Empire, could today fight against Great Britain if war breaks out. Moreover, as I mentioned earlier, even some small countries have acquired nuclear weapons.

What causes great fear is the knowledge that such nuclear weapons could end up in the hands of such people who either do not have the ability or who choose not to think about the consequences of their actions. In truth, such people do not even care about the consequences, and are trigger-happy.

Thus, if the major powers do not act with justice, do not eliminate the frustrations of smaller nations and do not adopt great and wise policies, then the situation will spiral out of control and the destruction that will follow is beyond our comprehension and imagination. Even the majority of the world who do desire peace will also become engulfed by this devastation.

Thus, it is my ardent wish and hope that the leaders of all major nations come to understand this dreadful reality, and so instead of adopting aggressive policies and utilising force to achieve their aims and objectives, they strive to adopt policies that promote and secure justice.

Recently, a very senior Russian military commander issued a serious warning about the potential risk of a nuclear war. It was his view that such a war would not be fought in Asia or elsewhere, but would be fought on Europe's borders, and that the threat might originate and ignite from Eastern European countries. Though some people will say that this was simply his personal opinion, I myself do not believe his views to be improbable, but in addition, I also believe that if such a war breaks out, then it is highly likely that Asian countries will also become involved.

Another news item that was recently given widespread media coverage was the views of a recently retired chief of Israel's intelligence agency, Mossad. During an interview with the well-known American television channel, CBS, he said that it was becoming apparent that the Israeli Government wished to wage war on Iran. He said that if such an attack took place it would be impossible to know where or how such a war would come to end. Thus, he strongly advised against any attack.

In this respect, it is my opinion that such a war will end with nuclear destruction.

I recently also came across an article in which the author stated that the situation of the world today is similar to the situation in 1932, both in economic terms and also politically. He wrote that in certain countries the people held no confidence in their politicians or their so-called democracies. He also said that there were many other similarities and parallels which were combining together to form the same image today that was witnessed just prior to the outbreak of the Second World War.

Some may disagree with his analysis, but on the contrary, I agree with it and that is why I believe the world's governments ought to be extremely worried and concerned at the current state of affairs. Similarly, the unjust leaders of some Muslim countries, whose only objective is to hold onto their power at any means and at any cost, should come to their senses. Otherwise, their acts and their foolishness will be the means of their demise, and they will lead their respective countries towards a most terrifying predicament.

We, who are members of the Aḥmadiyya Muslim Community, try our utmost to save the world and humanity from destruction. This is because in this era, we have accepted the Imam of the Age, who was sent by Allah as the Promised Messiah, and came as a servant to the Holy Prophet Muhammad (peace be upon him), who himself was sent as a Mercy for all of Mankind.

It is because we follow the teachings of the Holy Prophet (peace be upon him) that we feel extreme pain and anguish in our hearts at the state of the world. It is that pain which drives us in our efforts to try and save humanity from destruction and suffering. Therefore, I and all other Ahmadi Muslims are striving to fulfil our responsibilities towards achieving peace in the world.

One way in which I have tried to promote peace is through a series of letters that I have written to certain world leaders. A few months ago, I sent a letter to Pope Benedict, which was delivered to him in person by an Ahmadi representative of mine. In the letter I said to him that as he was the leader of the world's biggest religious denomination, he ought to endeavour to establish peace.

In similar vein, more recently and upon observing that hostilities between Iran and Israel were boiling over to a very dangerous level, I sent a letter to both Israel's Prime Minister, Benjamin Netanyahu, and Iran's President, Mahmud Ahmedinejad, in which I urged them to forsake all forms of haste and recklessness when making decisions, for the sake of mankind.

I have also recently written to President Barack Obama and Canada's Prime Minister, Stephen Harper, calling on both of them to fulfil their roles and responsibilities towards the development of peace and harmony in the world.

I am also planning to write and warn other Heads of State and leaders in the near future.

I do not know if my letters will be given any value or weight by the various leaders I have written to, but whatever their reaction, an attempt has been made by me, as the Khalīfah and spiritual leader of millions of Ahmadi Muslims worldwide, to convey their feelings and emotions about the perilous state of the world.

Let it be clear that I have not expressed these sentiments because of any personal fear, but instead, I am motivated out of a sincere love for humanity.

This love for humanity has been developed and instilled in all true Muslims by the teachings of the Holy Prophet Muhammad (peace be upon him) who, as I have already mentioned, was sent as a means of mercy and compassion for all of mankind.

Most likely you will be very surprised or even shocked to hear that our love for mankind is a direct result of the teachings of the Holy Prophet (peace be upon him). The question may arise in your minds, that why then are there Muslim terrorist groups that are killing innocent people, or why are there Muslim governments, who in order to protect their seats of power, are ordering the mass killings of members of their public?

Let it be absolutely clear that in reality, such evil acts are completely contrary to the real teachings of Islam. The Holy Qur'an does not give permission, under any circumstances, for extremism or terrorism.

In this age, according to our beliefs, God Almighty sent the Founder of the Aḥmadiyya Muslim Jamāʿat, Ḥaḍrat Mirza Ghulam Ahmad of Qadian (peace be upon him) as the Promised Messiah and the Imam Mahdi, in complete submission to the Holy Prophet Muhammad (peace be upon him). The Promised Messiah (peace be upon him) was sent to propagate the real and true teachings of Islam and the Holy Qur'an. He was sent to establish a bond between man and God Almighty. He was sent to identify and recognize the rights owed by man to one another. He was sent to end all forms of religious warfare. He was sent to establish the respect, dignity and honour of every Founder and every Prophet of any religion. He was sent to draw attention towards attaining the highest standards of moral values and to establish peace, love, compassion and brotherhood throughout the world.

If you go to any part of the world, you will find these very qualities embedded in all true Ahmadi Muslims. For us neither terrorists nor extremists are examples, nor are the cruel Muslim dictators examples to us, nor are Western powers examples to us. The example that we follow is that of the Founder of Islam, the Holy Prophet Muhammad (peace be upon him) and our guiding instructions are the Holy Qur'an.

Thus, from this Peace Symposium, I send a message to the entire world, that the message and teachings of Islam are of love, compassion, kindness and peace.

Sadly, we find that a small minority of Muslims present a completely distorted image of Islam and act upon their misguided beliefs. I say to all of you, that you should not believe this to be the real Islam and thus use such misguided acts as a licence to hurt the sentiments of the peaceful majority of Muslims or make them a target of cruelty.

The Holy Qur'an is the holiest and most sacred Book for all Muslims and so to use abusive and foul language or to burn it will certainly grievously injure the feelings of Muslims. We have seen that when this happens it often leads to a completely wrong and inappropriate reaction by extremist Muslims.

Just very recently we heard of two incidents in Afghanistan, where some American soldiers disrespected the Holy Qur'an, and killed innocent women and children in their homes. Similarly, a merciless person shot dead some French soldiers in the South of France without any reason, and then some days later he entered a school and killed three innocent Jewish children and one of their teachers.

We find that this behaviour is completely wrong and can never lead to peace. We also see such cruelties regularly come to pass in Pakistan and elsewhere and so all of these acts are giving the opponents of Islam fuel to vent their hatred and a pretext upon which to pursue their goals on a large scale. Such barbaric acts carried out on a smaller scale are not conducted due to personal enmities or grudges, but are in fact the result of the unjust policies adopted by certain governments, both at a domestic and at an international level.

Thus, for peace in the world to be established it is essential that proper standards of justice are developed at every level, and in every country of the world. The Holy Qur'an has deemed the killing of one innocent person without reason akin to killing all of mankind.

So once again, as a Muslim, I shall make it absolutely clear that Islam does not permit cruelty or oppression in any way, shape or form. This is an injunction that is absolute and without exception. The Qur'an further states that even if any country or people hold enmity towards you, that must not stop you from acting in a fully just and fair manner when dealing with them. It should not be that any enmities or rivalries lead you to taking revenge or acting disproportionately. Another vital injunction given to us by the Holy Qur'an is that the wealth and resources of others should not be looked upon with envy or greed.

I have mentioned just a few points, but these are such that are crucially important because they lay the foundation for peace and justice in society and the wider world. I pray that the world pays attention to these key issues, so that we can be saved from the destruction of the world that we are being led towards by the unjust and untruthful people.

I would like to take this opportunity to apologize that I have taken up quite some time, but the truth is that the subject of establishing peace in the world is of truly vast importance.

Time is running out, and before it is too late we must all pay great heed and attention to the needs of the time.

Before I bring my speech to an end, I would like to talk about one important thing. As we are all aware, these days the Diamond Jubilee of Her Majesty, Queen Elizabeth II, is being celebrated. If we rewind the clock 115 years to 1897, the Diamond Jubilee of Queen Victoria was also being celebrated. At that time, the Founder of the Aḥmadiyya Muslim Community sent a congratulatory message to Queen Victoria.

In his message, he conveyed both the teachings of Islam and he also sent a message of prayers for the British Government and for the long life of the Queen. In his message, the Promised Messiah (peace be upon him) wrote that the best quality of the Queen's Government was that under its rule, all people were granted religious freedom.

In today's world the British Government no longer rules over the Sub-Continent, but still the principles of freedom of religion are deeply entrenched in British society and its laws, through which every person is granted religious freedom.

Indeed, a very beautiful example of this freedom is being witnessed here tonight where the followers of various different faiths, religions and beliefs have joined together in one place with a common aspiration of seeking peace in the world.

Therefore, using the same words and prayers that the Promised Messiah (peace be upon him) used, I take this opportunity to offer heartfelt congratulations to Queen Elizabeth. As he said:

> May our congratulations filled with happiness and gratitude to our compassionate Queen be conveyed. And may the honourable Queen always be kept happy and content.

The Promised Messiah (peace be upon him) further offered

prayers for Queen Victoria, and so again I use his words to pray for Queen Elizabeth:

> O Powerful and Noble God. Through your Grace and Blessings keep our honoured Queen forever happy in the same way that we are living happily under her benevolence and kindness; and be kind and loving to her in the same way that we are living in peace and prosperity under her generous and righteous rule.

Thus, these are sentiments of gratitude that are held by every Ahmadi Muslim who is a British citizen.

At the end I would like to once again express my gratitude to all of you from the depths of my heart, who by coming here have demonstrated their love, affection and brotherhood.

Thank you very much.

THE PATH TO PEACE—
JUST RELATIONS BETWEEN NATIONS

CAPITOL HILL
WASHINGTON, D.C., USA, 2012

The first Muslim Congressman, Keith Ellison meeting Ḥaḍrat Khalīfatul-Masīḥ V[aba]

Brad Sherman (Democratic member of the United States House of Representatives) presenting American flag to Ḥaḍrat Khalīfatul-Masīḥ V[aba]

Ḥaḍrat Mirza Masroor Ahmad, Khalīfatul-Masīḥ V[aba] delivers his keynote address at U.S. Capitol Hill

Ḥaḍrat Mirza Masroor Ahmad, Khalīfatul-Masīḥ V[aba] leading silent prayer at U.S. Capitol Hill

...aḍrat Khalīfatul-Masīḥ V[aba] during his
...ficial tour of U.S. Capitol Hill

...aḍrat Khalīfatul-Masīḥ V[aba] in U.S. Capitol Hill
...ter his historic address to the US Statesmen
...nd Bureaucrats

Preface

On June 27, 2012, a historic event took place at Capitol Hill in Washington, D.C. Ḥaḍrat Khalīfatul-Masīḥ V^{aba}, Fifth Successor to the Promised Messiah^{as} and Head of the Ahmadiyya Muslim Community, addressed leading congressmen, senators, ambassadors, White House and State Department Staff, NGO leaders, religious leaders, professors, policy advisors, bureaucrats, members of the Diplomatic Corps, representatives of think-tanks and the Pentagon and journalists from the media. The meeting, the first of its kind, gave the opportunity to some of the most influential leaders in the United States, including Honourable Nancy Pelosi, the Democratic Leader in the House of Representatives, to hear first-hand Islam's message on world peace. Following the event, His Holiness was given a tour of the Capitol Hill building, before being escorted to the House of Representatives where a Resolution was introduced in honour of his visit to the United States.

The introductory paragraph of the Resolution stated:

> Welcoming His Holiness, Ḥaḍrat Mirza Masroor Ahmad, the worldwide spiritual and administrative head of the Ahmadiyya Muslim Community, to Washington, DC, and recognizing his commitment to world peace, justice, nonviolence, human rights, religious freedom and democracy...

The full list of attendees at the Capitol Hill event reads as follows:

- U.S. Senator Robert Casey, Sr. (Democrat Pennsylvania)
- U.S. Senator John Cornyn (Republican Texas)
- Democratic Leader Nancy Pelosi (Democrat California)
- U.S. Congressman Keith Ellison (Democrat Minnesota)
- U.S. Congressman Bradley Sherman (Democrat California)
- U.S. Congressman Frank Wolf (Republican Virginia)
- U.S. Congressman Michael Honda (Democrat California)
- U.S. Congressman Timothy Murphy (Republican Pennsylvania)
- U.S. Congresswoman Jeannette Schmidt (Republican Ohio)
- U.S. Congresswoman Janice Hahn (Democrat California)
- U.S. Congresswoman Janice Schakowsky (Democrat Illinois)
- U.S. Congresswoman Jackie Speier (Democrat California)
- U.S. Congresswoman Zoe Lofgren (Democrat California)

- U.S. Congresswoman Sheila Jackson Lee (Democrat Texas)
- U.S. Congressman Gary Peters (Democrat Michigan)
- U.S. Congressman Thomas Petri (Republican Wisconsin)
- U.S. Congressman Adam Schiff (Democrat California)
- U.S. Congressman Michael Capuano (Democrat Massachusetts)
- U.S. Congressman Howard Berman (Democrat California)
- U.S. Congresswoman Judy Chu (Democrat California)
- U.S. Congressman André Carson (Democrat Indiana)
- U.S. Congresswoman Laura Richardson (Democrat California
- U.S. Congressman Lloyd Poe (Republican Texas)
- U.S. Congressman Barney Frank (Democrat Massachusetts)
- U.S. Congressman. Bruce Braley (Democrat Iowa)
- U.S. Congressman Dennis Kucinich (Democrat Ohio)
- U.S. Congressman Trent Franks (Republican Arizona)
- U.S. Congressman Chris Murphy (Democrat Connecticut)
- U.S. Congressman Hank Johnson (Democrat Georgia)
- U.S. Congressman James Clyburn (Democrat South Carolina)
- His Excellency Bockari Kortu Stevens, Ambassador of Sierra Leone to the United States

- Dr. Katrina Lantos Swett, Chairwoman, United States Commission on International Religious Freedom

- Hon. Tim Kaine, Former Governor of Virginia

- Amb. Susan Burk, Special Representative of President Barack Obama for Nuclear Nonproliferation

- Amb. Suzan Johnson Cook, U.S. Ambassador at Large for International Religious Freedom

- Hon. Khaled Aljalahma, Deputy Chief of Mission, Embassy of the Kingdom of Bahrain to the United States

- Rev. Monsignor Jean-Francois Lantheaume, First Counselor (Deputy Chief of Mission), The Apostolic Nunciature of the Holy See to the United States

- Ms. Sara Al-Ojaili, Public Affairs/Liaison Officer, Embassy of the Sultanate of Oman to the United States

- Mr. Salim Al Kindie, First Secretary, Embassy of the Sultanate of Oman to the United States

- Ms. Fozia Fayyaz, Embassy of Pakistan to the United States

- Hon. Saida Zaid, Counselor, Embassy of Morocco to the United States

- Hon. Nabeel Munir, Minister-IV (Security Council), Pakistan Permanent Mission to the United Nations

- Hon. Josef Renggli, Minister-Counselor, Embassy of Switzerland to the United States

- Hon. Alyssa Ayres, Deputy Assistant Secretary for South and Central Asia, U.S. Department of State

- Amb. Karl Inderfurth, Senior Adviser and Wadhwani Chair in U.S.-India Policy Studies, Center for Strategic and International Studies

- Hon. Donald A. Camp, Senior Associate, Center for Strategic and International Studies

- Amb. Jackie Wolcott, Executive Director, U.S. Commission on International Religious Freedom

- Dr. Azizah al-Hibri, Commissioner, U.S. Commission on International Religious Freedom

- Mr. Isaiah Leggett, County Executive, Montgomery Count, Maryland

- Ms. Victoria Alvarado, Director, Office of International Religious Freedom, U.S. Department of State

- Dr. Imad Dean Ahmad, Director, Minaret of Freedom Institute

- Dr. Zainab Alwani, Assistant Professor of Islamic Studies, Howard University School of Divinity

- Ms. Deborah L. Benedict, Associate Counsel, U.S. Citizenship and Immigration Services, Department of Homeland Security

- Ms. Lora Berg, Senior Adviser to Special Representative to Muslim Communities, U.S. Department of State

- Dr. Charles Butterworth, Professor (Emeritus) of Government and Politics, University of Maryland, College Park

- Father John Crossin, Executive Director for Secretariat for Ecumenical and Interreligious Affairs, United States Conference of Catholic Bishops

- Major (Ret.) Franz Gayl, Senior Science Adviser, U.S. Marine Corps.

- Dr. Sue Gurawadena-Vaughn, Director of International Religious Freedom and South East Asia Programs, Freedom House

- Mr. Frank Jannuzi, Head of Washington Office, Amnesty International USA

- Mr. T. Kumar, International Advocacy Director, Amnesty International USA

- George Leventhal, Member of the Montgomery County Council

- Mr. Amer Latif, Visiting Fellow, Wadhwani Chair in U.S.-India Policy Studies, Center for Strategic and International Studies

- Mr. Tim Lenderking, Director of Pakistan Affairs, U.S. State Department

- Mr. Jalal Malik, International Affairs Officer, U.S. Army National Guard

- Mr. Naveed Malik, Foreign Service Officer, U.S. Department of State

- Ms. Dalia Mogahed, Senior Analyst and Executive Director, Gallup Center for Muslim Studies

- Mr. Paul Monteiro, Associate Director, White House Office of Public Engagement

- Major General David Quantock, United States Army Provost General

- Ms. Tina Ramirez, Director of International and Government Relations, The Becket Fund

- Rabbi David Saperstein, Director and Counsel, Religious Action Center for Reform Judaism

- Chaplain, Brigadier General Alphonse Stephenson, Director of the National Guard Bureau Office of the Chaplain

- Mr. Knox Thames, Director of Policy and Research, U.S. Commission on International Religious Freedom

- Mr. Eric Treene, Special Counsel for Religious Discrimination, Civil Rights Division, U.S. Department of Justice

- Dr. Hassan Abbas, Professor, Regional and Analytical Studies Department, National Defense University

- Mr. Malik Siraj Akbar, Reagan-Fascell Fellow, National Endowment for Democracy

- Mr. Matthew K. Asada, Congressional Fellow to Rep. Gary Peters

- Ms. Stacy Burdett, Director of Government and National Affairs, Anti-Defamation League

- Ms. Elizabeth Cassidy, Deputy Director for Policy and Research, U.S. Commission on International Religious Freedom

- Ms. Aimee Chiu, Director of Media, Communication, and Public Relations, American Islamic Congress

- Mr. Cornelius Cremin, Department of State, Bureau of Democracy, Human Rights and Labor, Acting Deputy Director and Foreign Affairs Officer for Pakistan

- Mr. Sadanand Dhume, Resident Fellow, American Enterprise Institute

- Dr. Richard Gathro, Dean of Nyack College, Washington D.C.

- Mr. Joe Grieboski, Chairman, The Institute on Religion and Public Policy
- Ms. Sarah Grieboski, The Institute on Religion and Public Policy
- Dr. Max Gross, Adjunct Professor, Prince Alwaleed Bin Talal Center for Muslim-Christian Understanding, Georgetown University
- Dr. Riaz Haider, Clinical Professor of Medicine, George Washington University
- Ms. Huma Haque, Assistant Director, South Asia Center, Atlantic Council
- Mr. Jay Kansara, Associate Director, Hindu American Foundation
- Mr. Hamid Khan, Senior Program Officer, Rule of Law Center, U.S. Institute for Peace
- Ms. Valerie Kirkpatrick, Associate for Refugees and U.S. Advocacy, Human Rights Watch
- Mr. Alex Kronemer, Unity Productions
- Mr. Paul Liben, Executive Writer, U.S. Commission on International Religious Freedom
- Ms. Amy Lillis, Foreign Affairs Officer, U.S. Department of State
- Mr. Graham Mason, Legislative Assistant to Rep. Allyson Schwartz
- Ms. Lauren Markoe, Religion News Service
- Mr. Dan Merica, CNN.com
- Mr. Joseph V. Montville, Senior Associate, Merrimack

College Center for the Study of Jewish-Christian-Muslim Relations

- Mr. Aaron Myers, Program Officer, Freedom House
- Ms. Attia Nasar, Regional Coordinating Officer, U.S. Department of State
- Ms. Melanie Nezer, Senior Director, US Policy and Advocacy, HIAS
- Dr. Elliott Parris, Bowie State University
- Mr. John Pinna, Director of Government and International Relations, American Islamic Congress
- Mr. Arif Rafiq, Adjunct Scholar, Middle East Institute
- Ms. Maya Rajaratnam, Amnesty International
- Ms. Rachel Sauer, Foreign Affairs Officer, U.S. Department of State
- Dr. Jerome Schiele, Dean of College of Professional Studies, Bowie State University
- Ms. Samantha Schnitzer, Staff, United States Commission on International Religious Freedom
- Dr. Mary Hope Schwoebel, Senior Program Officer, Academy for International Conflict Management and Peacebuilding, U.S. Institute for Peace
- Ms. Sarah Schlesinger, International and Government Relations Associate, The Becket Fund
- Dr. Frank Sellin, Kyrgystan Desk Officer, U.S. Department of State
- Ms. Anna-Lee Stangl, Christian Solidarity Worldwide

- Ms. Kalinda Stephenson, Professional Staff, Tom Lantos Human Rights Commission
- Mr. Jordan Tama, Lead Democratic Staffer, Tom Lantos Human Rights Commission
- Mr. Shaun Tandon, AFP
- Dr. Wilhelmus Valkenberg, Professor of Religion and Culture, The Catholic University of America
- Mr. Anthony Vance, Director of External Affairs, Baha'is of the United States
- Mr. Jihad Saleh Williams, Government Affairs Representative, Islamic Relief USA
- Ms. Amelia Wang, Chief of Staff to Congresswoman Judy Chu
- Ms. Moh Sharma, Legislative Fellow to Congresswoman Judy Chu

U.S. Congress—House Resolution 709

112TH CONGRESS
2D SESSION
H. RES. 709

Welcoming His Holiness, Hadhrat Mirza Masroor Ahmad, the worldwide spiritual and administrative head of the Ahmadiyya Muslim Community, to Washington, DC, and recognizing his commitment to world peace, justice, nonviolence, human rights, religious freedom, and democracy.

IN THE HOUSE OF REPRESENTATIVES

JUNE 27, 2012

Ms. ZOE LOFGREN of California (for herself, Mr. SHERMAN, Mr. CONNOLLY of Virginia, Mr. HINCHEY, Ms. ESHOO, Ms. SPEIER, Ms. RICHARDSON, Mr. SCHIFF, Ms. SCHAKOWSKY, Mr. HONDA, Mr. WOLF, Mr. PETERS, Mr. DENT, Ms. CHU, Mr. BERMAN, Mr. FRANKS of Arizona, Ms. JACKSON LEE of Texas, Ms. SCHWARTZ, Mr. BRALEY of Iowa, and Mr. McGOVERN) submitted the following resolution; which was referred to the Committee on Foreign Affairs

---

RESOLUTION

Welcoming His Holiness, Hadhrat Mirza Masroor Ahmad, the worldwide spiritual and administrative head of the Ahmadiyya Muslim Community, to Washington, DC, and recognizing his commitment to world peace, justice, nonviolence, human rights, religious freedom, and democracy.

Whereas, from June 16, 2012, to July 2, 2012, His Holiness, Hadhrat Mirza Masroor Ahmad, the worldwide spiritual and administrative head of the Ahmadiyya Muslim Community, an international religious organization with mil-

2

lions of members across the globe, is making a historic visit to the United States;

Whereas His Holiness was elected to become fifth Khalifa to Mirza Ghulam Ahmad, a lifelong position, on April 22, 2003;

Whereas His Holiness is a leading Muslim figure promoting peace, who in his sermons, lectures, books, and personal meetings has continually advocated the Ahmadiyya values of service to humanity, universal human rights, and a peaceful and just society;

Whereas the Ahmadiyya Muslim Community has suffered repeated hardships, including discrimination, persecution, and violence;

Whereas, on May 28, 2010, 86 Ahmadi Muslims were killed in Lahore, Pakistan, when two mosques belonging to the Ahmadiyya Muslim Community were attacked by anti-Ahmadiyya terrorists;

Whereas despite the continued sectarian persecution that Ahmadi Muslims are subjected to, His Holiness continues to forbid violence;

Whereas His Holiness has traveled globally to promote and facilitate service to humanity, meeting with presidents, prime ministers, parliamentarians, and ambassadors of state;

Whereas during his visit to the United States, His Holiness will meet thousands of American Muslims in addition to significant United States Government leaders in order to strengthen relationships and find means of establishing peace and justice for all people; and

Whereas, on the morning of June 27, 2012, His Holiness will deliver the keynote address at a special bipartisan recep-

•HRES 709 IH

3

tion at the Rayburn House Office Building on Capitol Hill, "The Path to Peace: Just Relations Between Nations": Now, therefore, be it

1   *Resolved,* That the House of Representatives—

2   (1) welcomes His Holiness, Mirza Masroor

3   Ahmad to Washington, DC;

4   (2) commends His Holiness for promoting indi-

5   vidual and world peace, as well as individual and

6   world justice; and

7   (3) commends His Holiness for his perseverance

8   in counseling Ahmadi Muslims to eschew any form

9   of violence, even in the face of severe persecution.

○

The Path to Peace—
Just Relations Between Nations

Bismillāhir-Raḥmānir-Raḥīm—In the name of Allah, the Gracious, Ever Merciful.

All distinguished guests—*assalāmo 'alaikum wa raḥmatullāhe wa barakātohū*—peace and blessings of Allah be upon you all.

Before proceeding, I would like to first of all take this opportunity to thank you all for taking the time to come and listen to what I have to say. I have been requested to speak about a subject that is extremely vast and wide ranging. It has many different aspects and therefore, it is not possible for me to cover all of them in the short time available. The subject that I have been asked to speak about is the establishment of world peace. Certainly, this is the most vital and pressing issue facing the world today. However, as the time is limited, I will only briefly give the Islamic viewpoint on the establishment of peace through just and equal relations between nations.

The truth is that peace and justice are inseparable—you cannot have one without the other. Certainly, this principle is something that all wise and intelligent people understand. Leaving aside those people who are determined to create disorder in the world, no one can ever claim that in any society, country or even the entire world, that there can be disorder or a lack of peace where justice and fair dealing exist. Nevertheless, we find in many parts of the world that disorder and a lack of peace are prevalent. Such disorder is visible both internally within countries, and externally in terms of the relations between various nations. Such disorder and strife exists even though all governments claim to make policies that are based on justice. All claim that the establishment of peace is their primary objective. Yet, in general, there is little doubt that restlessness and anxiety is increasing in the world, and so disorder is spreading. This clearly proves that somewhere along the line, the requirements of justice are not being fulfilled. Therefore, there is an urgent need to try and end inequality, wherever and whenever it exists. Thus, as the worldwide Head of the Ahmadiyya Muslim Community, I would like to make a few observations about the need for, and the ways to achieve peace based on justice.

The Ahmadiyya Muslim Community is purely a religious community. It is our firm belief that the Messiah and Reformer who was destined to appear in this age and enlighten the world as to Islam's true teachings has indeed arrived. We believe that the Founder of our Community, Ḥaḍrat Mirza Ghulam Ahmad[as] of Qadian, was that very Promised Messiah and Reformer, and thus we have accepted him. He pressed upon his followers to act and propagate the real and true teachings of Islam that are based on the Holy Qur'an. Therefore, everything that I will say in relation to establishing peace, and in relation to conducting just international relations, will be based on Qur'anic teachings.

In relation to achieving world peace, all of you regularly express your opinions, and indeed make great efforts. Your creative and intelligent minds allow you to present great ideas, plans and indeed a vision of peace. Thus, this issue does not require me to speak from a worldly or political perspective, but instead my entire focus will be based on how to establish peace based on religion. For this purpose I shall, as I have earlier said, present some very important guidelines based on the teachings of the Holy Qur'an.

It is important to always remember that human knowledge and intellect is not perfect, but is in fact limited. Thus, when making decisions or forming thoughts often certain factors enter human minds, which can cloud judgement and lead to a person trying to fulfil his own rights. Ultimately, this can lead to an unjust outcome and decision being made. God's Law, however, is perfect and so no vested interests or unfair provisions exist. This is because God only desires for the good and betterment of His Creation and therefore, His Law is based entirely on justice. The day the people of the world come to recognise and understand this crucial point will be the day that the foundation for true and everlasting peace will be laid. Otherwise, we continue to find that although efforts are endlessly made to establish world peace, yet they are unable to provide any worthwhile results.

After the conclusion of the First World War, the leaders of certain countries desired for good and peaceful relations between all nations in future. Thus, in an effort to achieve world peace the League of Nations was formed. Its principal aim was to maintain world peace and to prevent future wars from breaking out. Unfortunately, the rules of the League and the resolutions it passed had certain flaws and weaknesses and so they did not properly protect the rights of all peoples and all nations equally. Consequently, as a result of the inequalities that existed, long-term peace could not prevail. The efforts of the League failed and this led directly to World War II.

We are all aware of the unparalleled destruction and devastation that ensued, where around 75 million people globally lost their lives, many of who were innocent civilians. That war should have been more than enough to open the eyes of the world. It should have been a means to developing wise policies that granted all parties their due rights, based on justice, and thus prove to be a means of establishing peace in the world. The world's governments at the time did endeavour to some extent to try and establish peace, and hence the United Nations was established. However, it soon became quite apparent that the noble and over-arching objective underpinning the United Nations could not be fulfilled. Indeed, today certain governments quite openly make statements that prove its failure.

What does Islam say in relation to international relations that are based on justice, and so a means of establishing peace? In the Holy Qur'an, God Almighty has made it clear that whilst our nationalities or ethnic backgrounds act as a means of identity, they do not entitle or validate any form of superiority of any kind.*

The Qur'an, thus, makes clear that all people are born equal. Furthermore, in the final sermon ever delivered by the Holy Prophet Muhammad^sa, he instructed all Muslims to always

---

* ch. 49: v. 14

remember that an Arab is not superior to a non-Arab and nor is a non-Arab superior to an Arab. He taught that a white person is not superior to a black person and nor is a black person superior to a white person. Thus, it is a clear teaching of Islam that the people of all nationalities and all races are equal. It is also made clear that all people should be granted equal rights without any discrimination or prejudice. This is the key and golden principle that lays the foundation for harmony between different groups and nations, and for the establishment of peace.

However, today we find that there is division and separation between powerful and weaker nations. For example, in the United Nations we find that there is a distinction made between certain countries. Thus, in the Security Council there are some permanent members and some non-permanent members. This division has proved to be an internal source of anxiety and frustration and thus we regularly hear reports of certain countries protesting against this inequality. Islam teaches absolute justice and equality in all matters and so we find another very crucial guideline in Chapter 5, verse 3 of the Holy Qur'an. In this verse it states that to fully comply with the requirements of justice, it is necessary to treat even those people, who go beyond all limits in their hatred and enmity, with fairness and equity. The Qur'an teaches that wherever and whoever counsels you towards goodness and virtue, you should accept it, and wherever and whoever counsels you towards sinful or unjust behaviour, you should reject it.

A question that naturally arises is that what is the standard of justice required by Islam? In Chapter 4, verse 136, the Holy Qur'an states that even if you have to testify against yourself, or your parents or your most loved ones, then you must do so in order to uphold justice and to uphold the truth. Powerful and rich countries should not usurp the rights of the poor and weaker countries in an effort to preserve their own rights, and nor should they deal with the poorer nations in an unjust fashion. On the other hand, the poor and weaker nations should not seek to inflict harm on the powerful or wealthy nations whenever the opportunity arises. Instead, both sides should endeavour to fully abide by the principles of justice. Indeed, this is a matter of crucial importance in maintaining peaceful relations between countries.

Another requirement for peace between nations based on justice is given in Chapter 15, verse 89 of the Holy Qur'an where it states that no party should ever look enviously at the resources and wealth of others. Similarly, no country should seek to unjustly appropriate or take over the resources of another country on the false pretext of trying to assist or support them. Thus, on the basis of providing technical expertise, governments should not take advantage of other nations by making unjust trade deals or contracts. Similarly, on the basis of providing expertise or assistance, governments should not try to take control of the natural resources or assets of the developing nations. Where less educated people or governments need to be taught how to properly utilise their natural resources, then this should be done.

Then, nations and governments should always seek to serve and help those less fortunate. However, such service should not be rendered with an aim of achieving national or political benefits or as a means to fulfil vested interests. We find that in the past six or seven decades the United Nations has launched many programmes or foundations aiming to help the poor countries to progress. Towards this effort they have explored the natural resources of the developing nations. However, despite these efforts, none of the poorer countries have reached the stage or level of the developed nations. One reason for this is certainly wide-ranging corruption by many of the governments of those under-developed countries. With regret though I must say that despite this, as a means to further their own interests, the developed nations have continued to deal with such governments. Trade deals, international aid and business contracts have continued to be processed. As a result, the frustrations and restlessness of the poor and deprived segments of society have continued to increase and this has led to rebellion and internal disorder within those countries. The poor people of the developing countries have become so frustrated that they have turned against not only their own leaders, but also the big powers as well. This has played into the hands of the extremist groups, who have taken advantage of the frustrations, and so have been able to encourage such people towards joining their groups and supporting their hate-filled ideology. The ultimate result of this has been that the peace of the world has been destroyed.

Thus, Islam has drawn our attention to various means for peace. It requires absolute justice. It requires truthful testimony to always be given. It requires that our glances are not cast enviously in the direction of the wealth of others. It requires that the developed nations put aside their vested interests, and instead help and serve the less developed and poorer nations with a truly selfless attitude and spirit. If all of these factors are observed, then true peace will be established.

If despite all these aforementioned measures any country transgresses all limits and attacks another country, and seeks to unjustly take control of its resources, then other countries should certainly take measures to stop such cruelty—but they should always act with justice when doing so.

The circumstances for taking action, based on Islamic teachings are detailed in the Qur'an, in Chapter 49.* It teaches that when two nations are in dispute and this leads to war, then other governments should strongly counsel them towards dialogue and diplomacy so that they can come to an agreement and reconciliation on the basis of a negotiated settlement. If, however, one of the parties does not accept the terms of agreement and wages war, then other countries should unite together and fight to stop that aggressor. When the aggressive nation is defeated and agrees to mutual negotiation, then all parties should work towards an agreement that leads to long-standing peace and reconciliation. Harsh and unjust conditions should not be enforced that leads to the hands of any nation being tied, because in the long-term that will lead to restlessness, which will ferment and spread. The result of such restlessness will be further disorder.

In circumstances where a third-party government seeks to bring about reconciliation between two parties, then it should act with sincerity and total impartiality. This impartiality should remain even if one of the parties speaks against it. Therefore, the third-party should display no anger in such circumstances, it should seek no revenge, nor should it act in an unfair manner. All parties should be afforded their due rights.

Thus, for the requirements of justice to be fulfilled, it is essential that the countries that are negotiating a settlement should themselves not seek to fulfil their own personal interests, nor try

---

*   ch. 49: v.10

to derive benefit unduly from either country. They should not interfere unjustly or pressure either of the parties unfairly. The natural resources of any country should not be taken advantage of. Unnecessary and unfair restrictions should not be placed upon such countries, because this is neither just and nor can it ever prove to be a source of improving relations between countries.

Due to time constraints, I have only very briefly mentioned these points. In short, if we desire for peace to be established in the world, then we must leave aside our personal and national interests for the greater good and instead we must establish mutual relations that are based entirely on justice. Otherwise, some of you might agree with me that due to alliances, blocs may be formed in future—or I can even say they have started forming—and it is not unlikely that disorder will continue to increase in the world, which will ultimately lead to a huge destruction. The effects of such devastation and warfare will surely last for many generations. Therefore, the United States, as the world's largest power, should play its role in acting with true justice and with such good intentions, as I have described. If it does so then the world will always remember with great admiration your great efforts. It is my prayer that this becomes a reality.

Thank you very much. Thank you again.

According to our tradition, at the end of the function we normally perform a silent prayer. Thus, I will perform the silent prayer and the Ahmadis will follow me. All of you, our guests, can pray in your own way.

THE KEY TO PEACE— GLOBAL UNITY

EUROPEAN PARLIAMENT
BRUSSELS, BELGIUM, 2012

Ḥaḍrat Khalīfatul-Masīḥ V^aba being welcomed by Martin Schulz, President of European Parliament

His Holiness leading silent prayer at conclusion of the European Parliament event.
Seated to his right: Dr. Charles Tannock (MEP-UK), left: Rafiq Hayat (National Amir AMA UK)

Ḥaḍrat Mirza Masroor Ahmad, Khalifatul-Masīḥ V^aba delivers the keynote address at the European Parliament event

...ss Conference with Ḥaḍrat Khalīfatul-Masīḥ V[aba] at European Parliament.
...ated with His Holiness is Dr. Charles Tannock (MEP-UK and Chair
...European Parliament Friends of Ahmadiyya Muslims Group)

...nne Kelam (MEP Estonia & Vice-Chair of
...ropean Parliament Friends of Ahmadiyya
...slims Group) meeting with His Holiness

Phil Bennion (MEP West Midlands and
member of European Parliament's South Asia
Delegation) meeting with His Holiness

Preface

On 3rd and 4th December 2012, Ḥaḍrat Khalīfatul-Masīḥ V[aba], Fifth Successor to the Promised Messiah[as] and worldwide Head of the Ahmadiyya Muslim Community, made his first visit to the European Parliament in Brussels where he delivered a historic keynote address to a packed audience of more than 350 guests representing 30 countries. The event was hosted by the newly launched cross-party European Parliament "Friends of Ahmadiyya Muslims" Group, chaired by Dr. Charles Tannock (MEP-UK). This is a cross-party and pan-European group of MEPs that has been set up to promote in the European Parliament the Ahmadiyya Muslim Community and advance their interests in Europe and the rest of the world. During the visit, Ḥaḍrat Mirza Masroor Ahmad[aba] also had a number of meetings with parliamentarians and dignitaries. Those he met included:

Dr. Charles Tannock (MEP-UK)—Member of the European

Parliament Foreign Affairs Committee, Member of the Sub-Committee on Human Rights, Vice-Chair of the Parliamentary Delegation for relations with the NATO Parliamentary Assembly and Chair of the European Parliament Friends of Ahmadiyya Muslims Group.

Tunne Kelam (MEP-Estonia)—Member of the European Parliament's Foreign Affairs Committee, the Sub-Committee on Security and Defence and Vice-Chair of the European Parliament Friends of Ahmadiyya Muslims Group.

Claude Moraes (MEP-UK)—Vice-Chair of the Delegation for Relations with the Arab Peninsula, Member of the Committee on Civil Liberties, Justice and Home Affairs, Deputy Leader of the European Parliamentary Labour Party and Vice-Chair of the European Parliament Friends of Ahmadiyya Muslims Group.

Barbara Lochbihler (MEP-Germany)—Chair of the European Parliament Sub-Committee on Human Rights.

Jean Lambert (MEP-UK)—Chair of the European Parliament South Asia Delegation.

Phil Bennion (MEP-UK)—Member of the European Parliament South Asia Delegation and Chairman of the LibDem European Group.

On 4th December, an international press conference was held in the Press Room of the European Parliament prior to the main event and a keynote address by His Holiness. His Holiness answered questions from a range of media outlets during a forty-minute press conference, attended by journalists and media organisations from UK, Spain, France, Belgium, Pakistan and other countries. In response to a question from the BBC about Islam's role in the world, His Holiness said, "Islam's message of peace is universal, which is why our motto is Love for All, Hatred for None." Responding to a question from a representative of the Spanish media, His Holiness said that all of the major religions in their original form taught a message of peace and so true Muslims believed in all of the Prophets. Each Prophet, he said, brought the message that there is One God. In response to a question from a representative of Malta's media, His Holiness said that the duty of Ahmadi Muslims was to bring mankind closer to God and to make the people of the world aware of their duty to safeguard each other's rights.

The main event was held before a packed audience. The Chair and Vice-Chairs of the European Parliament Friends of Ahmadiyya Muslims Group all took to the stage to welcome Ḥaḍrat Mirza Masroor Ahmad[aba], Head of the worldwide Ahmadiyya Muslim Community. Martin Schulz, MEP and President of the European Parliament, also made a special visit to meet with His Holiness. Before the keynote address by His Holiness, a number of MEPs addressed the audience and spoke of their admiration of peaceful Islam as advocated by the Ahmadiyya Muslim Jamā'at. Dr Charles Tannock MEP, Chair of the European Parliament Friends of Ahmadiyya Muslims Group, said "Ahmadi Muslims are a welcome example of tolerance in the world."

We present here the historic keynote address delivered by Ḥaḍrat Mirza Masroor Ahmad[aba], Khalīfatul-Masīḥ, Head of the world-wide Ahmadiyya Muslim Community.

The Key to Peace—Global Unity

Bismillāhir-Raḥmānir-Raḥīm—In the name of Allah, the Gracious, Ever Merciful.

All distinguished guests—*assalāmo ʿalaikum wa raḥmatullāhe wa barakātohū*—peace and blessings of Allah be upon you all.

First of all I would like to thank the organisers of this event who have given me the opportunity to speak to all of you here at the European Parliament. I would also like to thank all of the delegates, representing different countries, and other guests, who have gone to great efforts to come and attend this event.

Those people who are well-acquainted with the Ahmadiyya Muslim Jamāʿat—or Community—or even those who are less well-acquainted and who have contact with individual Ahmadis, will be fully aware that as a Community we constantly draw the attention of the world towards the establishment of peace and security. Certainly, we make full efforts within our resources towards achieving these goals.

As the Head of the Ahmadiyya Muslim Jamāʿat, I regularly speak about such matters whenever the opportunity arises. The fact that I speak about the need for peace and mutual love is not because of any new teaching brought by the Ahmadiyya Community. Whilst it is certainly true that to bring peace and reconciliation was one of the major objectives of the advent of the Founder of the Ahmadiyya Muslim Community, the reality is that all of our acts are due to the teachings that were revealed to the Founder of Islam, the Holy Prophet Muhammad[sa].

In the 1400 years following the time of the Holy Prophet[sa], the pure teachings he had brought had, unfortunately, been long forgotten by the majority of Muslims. Thus, in order to rejuvenate the true Islam, Allah the Almighty sent the Founder of the Ahmadiyya Muslim Community, Ḥaḍrat Mirza Ghulam Ahmad[as] of Qadian, in accordance with the prophecy of the Holy Prophet[sa] of Islam. I would request all of you to keep this point in mind when I come to speak about Islam's teachings in relation to the development of peace and harmony in the world.

I should also mention that there are multiple aspects of 'peace' and 'security'. As every individual facet is important in its own right, at the same time the way each aspect interlinks is also extremely important. For example, the basic building block for peace in society is tranquillity and harmony within the family home. The situation within a home is not limited, but has a knock-on effect on the peace of the local area, which in turn affects the peace of the wider town or city. If there is disturbance in the home it will negatively affect the local area and that will affect the town or city.

In the same way, the state of the town or city affects the peace of the entire country and ultimately the state of a nation affects the peace and harmony of the region or the entire world. Therefore, it is clear that if you wish to discuss even a single aspect of peace, you will find that its scope is not limited, but will continue to expand. In a similar way, we find that where there is a lack of peace, different methods are required to solve the issue, based on the underlying problems that exist and upon the particular aspects of peace and security that have been violated. When we bear this in mind, it is obvious that to fully discuss and address these issues in detail requires much more time than is currently available. Nevertheless, I will try to cover at least some aspects of Islam's true teachings.

In the modern world we find that many objections are raised against Islam and much of the blame for the disorder and strife in the world is attributed to the religion. Such allegations are made even though the very meanings of the word Islam are 'peace' and 'security'. Furthermore, Islam is that religion which has given specific guidance on how to establish peace and has laid down certain rules to achieve this. Before I go on to present to you a picture of Islam's true and peaceful teachings, I would like to briefly discuss the current state of the world. I am sure you will be well versed in these matters already, but I will raise them so that you are able to keep them in view when I come to discuss Islam's teachings about peace and harmony. We are all aware and accept that today's world has become like a global village. We are all connected through various means, whether it be through the modern modes of transport, whether it be through the media and Internet or through various other means. All of these factors have resulted in the nations of the world becoming closer together than ever before.

We find that in major countries people of all races, religions and nationalities have settled and are living together. Indeed, in many countries there is a significant population of foreign immigrants. The immigrants have become so well-embedded that it would be extremely difficult, or even impossible, for governments or the local people to remove them now. Although attempts have been made to curtail immigration and certain restrictions have been implemented, there are still various means through which a citizen of one nation is able to enter another country. Indeed, leaving aside illegal immigration, we find that certain international laws exist that assist those who are forced to migrate for certain genuine reasons.

We also find that as a result of mass immigration, restlessness and anxiety are spreading in certain countries. The responsibility for this lies with both parties—the immigrants and the local people. On the one hand some immigrants provoke the locals by refusing to integrate to any degree, whilst on the other hand some of the locals are displaying a lack of tolerance and open-heartedness. From time to time the hatred boils over to a very dangerous extent. In particular, hatred or enmity on the part of the locals in Western countries is often manifested towards Islam in reaction to the negative behaviour of certain Muslims, especially immigrants. The anger and reaction is not just on a small scale, but can and does reach extreme heights, which is why Western leaders regularly speak about those problems. Therefore, we find that on occasion, the German Chancellor speaks about Muslims being a part of Germany; we find that the Prime Minister of the United Kingdom speaks of the need for Muslims to integrate and the leaders of some countries have gone as far as to give warnings to the Muslims. The internal state of conflicts, if not worsening, at least has become of some concern. These matters might heat up and may lead to the destruction of peace. There should be no doubt that the effect of such conflicts will not be limited to the West but will impact the entire world, especially the Muslim countries. It will cause the relationship between the Western and Eastern World to severely deteriorate. Therefore, to improve the situation and for peace to develop, requires all parties to work together. Governments need to make policies that establish and protect mutual respect, through which hurting the sentiments of others or causing them any type of harm should be outlawed.

With regard to the immigrants, they must enter with a willingness to integrate with the local people, whilst the locals should be ready to open their hearts and display tolerance. Furthermore, simply to enforce certain restrictions against Muslims will not lead to peace, because they alone cannot change people's minds and views. This is not specific to Muslims, but whenever any person is forcibly suppressed due to his religion or belief, it will lead to a negative reaction through which peace will be severely harmed. As I have already said, we find that in certain countries conflicts are increasing, in particular between the local people and Muslim immigrants. It is apparent that both sides are becoming less tolerant and there is a reluctance to get to know one another. The European leadership needs to accept that this is the reality and understand it has a responsibility to establish mutual religious respect and tolerance. This is essential so that within every European country, and between European and Muslim countries, an atmosphere of goodwill develops so that the peace of the world is not shattered.

I believe that the cause of such conflicts and divisions is not only religion or beliefs and it is not merely a question of differences between Western and Muslim nations. In fact, a major root cause of the discord has been the global financial crisis. When there was no recession or credit crunch, nobody ever bothered about the influx of immigrants; Muslims or non-Muslims or Africans. However, the situation is now different and that has caused all this. It has even affected the mutual relationships of European countries, and so anger and resentment between the people of certain European nations and the people of other European countries is increasing daily. This state of despair is visible everywhere.

The formation of the European Union has been a great achievement on the part of European countries, for it has been a means of uniting the Continent. Thus, you should make all possible efforts to preserve this unity, by honouring each other's rights. The fears and worries held by members of the general public must be removed. To protect each other's society, you should be willing to accept fair and just demands of one another, and of course, there should be fair and just demands by the people of each and every country.

Remember that the strength of Europe lies in it remaining united and together as one. Such unity will not only benefit you here in Europe, but at a global level will be the means for this Continent to maintain its strength and influence. In fact, speaking from an Islamic perspective, we should strive for the entire world to unite together. In terms of currency, the world should be united. In terms of free business and trade, the world should be united and in terms of freedom of movement and immigration, cohesive and practical policies should be developed, so that the world can become united. In essence countries should seek to cooperate with one another so that division is replaced by unity. If these measures are taken then it will soon become apparent that the existing conflicts will end and be replaced by peace and mutual respect, provided true justice is practiced and each country realises its responsibility. It is with great regret that I must say that, although it is an Islamic teaching, the Islamic countries have been unable to unite amongst themselves. If they were able to cooperate and unite, then the Islamic countries would not need to constantly seek Western aid and help in order to alleviate their internal troubles and needs.

With these words, I shall now come to speak about true Islamic teachings in relation to the establishment of long lasting peace in the world. First of all, a fundamental and basic teaching of Islam is that a true Muslim is a person from whose tongue and hand all other peaceful people are safe. This is the definition of a Muslim given by the Holy Prophet Muhammad[sa]. After hearing this basic and beautiful principle, can any allegation or complaint be levelled against Islam? Certainly not. Islam teaches that only those who use their tongues and hands to spread injustice and hatred deserve to be punished. Thus, from a local level to a global level, if all parties remained within the confines of this golden principle we would find that there would never be religious disorder. There would never be political strife and nor would there be disorder based on greed and a desire to gain power. If these true Islamic principles are followed, then within countries, the members of the general public will safeguard each other's rights and feelings and the governments would fulfil their roles to protect all citizens.

At an international level each nation would work together with a spirit of true sympathy and compassion towards one another.

Another key principle Islam teaches is that, in an effort to develop peace, it is necessary for all parties to never display any form of pride or arrogance. This was perfectly illustrated by the Holy Prophet[sa] when he famously said a black person is not superior to a white person and nor is a white person superior to a black person. Neither is a European greater or superior to any other national, nor are Africans, Asians or the people of any other part of the world. Differences of nationality, colour or ethnicity act merely as a form of identity and recognition.

The truth is that in the modern world we all depend upon one another. Today even the major powers, like Europe or the United States, cannot survive by remaining completely isolated from all others. African countries cannot remain isolated and hope to flourish and neither can Asian countries or the people from any other part of the world. For example, if you want your economy to flourish, then you must be willing to embrace international trade. A clear example of how the world is now inter-linked is illustrated by the fact that the European or the world's financial crisis of the past few years has negatively affected, more or less, every country of the world. Furthermore, for countries to advance in science, or to excel in other fields of expertise, requires them to cooperate and help each other.

We should always remember that the people of the world, whether they are from Africa, Europe, Asia or anywhere else, have been given great intellectual capabilities by Allah the Almighty. If all parties utilise their God-given faculties to the best of their abilities for the betterment of mankind, then we will find that the world will become a haven of peace. However, if the developed nations try to suppress the growth and progress of the less developed or developing nations and do not give opportunities to the fertile and bright minds of those nations, then, no doubt, anxiety will spread and the ensuing restlessness will ruin international peace and security.

Another principle of Islam to develop peace is that we should not tolerate injustice towards others or for their rights to be usurped. In the same way that we would not accept for our own rights to be taken, we should not be willing to accept it for others. Islam teaches that where retribution is required then it must be proportionate to the act of transgression. However, if forgiveness can lead to reformation then the option to forgive should be taken. The true and overarching objectives should always be reformation, reconciliation and the development of long lasting peace. However, what in reality is happening today? If anyone commits a wrong or an injustice, then the victim seeks to extract revenge in a way which is completely out of proportion and far greater than the original injustice committed.

This is exactly what we are witnessing these days in the escalating conflict between Israel and Palestine. The major powers have openly expressed their outrage and concern at the situations in Syria, Libya or Egypt; even though it can be argued that they were, in essence, internal matters. Yet they do not seem to be concerned about, or that concerned about, the Palestinian people. This perceived double standard is causing grievances and malice to increase in the hearts of the people from Muslim countries against the major powers of the world. This anger and animosity is extremely dangerous and could boil over and explode at any time.

What will the result of that be? How much damage will be done to the developing world? Will they even be able to survive? How much will the developed nations be affected? Only God knows the answer to such questions. I cannot answer these and nobody can answer these. What we can be certain about is that the peace of the world will be destroyed.

Let it be clear that I am not speaking in support or favour of any particular individual country. What I wish to say is that all forms of cruelty, wherever they exist, must be eradicated and stopped regardless of whether they are perpetrated by the people of Palestine, the people of Israel or the people of any other country. The cruelties must be stopped, because if they are allowed to spread, then the flames of hatred will surely engulf the entire world to such an extent, that people will soon forget about the troubles caused by the current economic crisis. Instead, they will face a much more horrifying state of affairs. There will be such a huge loss of life that we cannot even comprehend or imagine.

Thus, it is the duty of the European countries, who suffered great losses during the Second World War, to learn from their past and save the world from destruction. To do this, they must fulfil the requirements of justice and be willing to accept their responsibilities. Islam strongly emphasises the need to always act in a fair and just manner. It teaches that no party should be given preferential treatment, or favoured unduly. It should be that a wrongdoer knows that if he tries to act unjustly towards any country, no matter its size or status, he will not be allowed to do so by the international community. If the member states of the United Nations, the countries that derive benefit from the European Union and the countries that are under the influence of the big powers or even the under developed countries all come to accept this, then and only then, peace can emerge.

Further, only if those nations who have veto power at the United Nations realise they will be held to account for their actions, can justice be truly established. In fact, I will go one step further and say that the right of veto power can never allow or facilitate the establishment of peace, because clearly not all countries are at an equal level. This is a point I also made earlier this year when I addressed leading politicians and policy makers of the United States, at Capitol Hill. If we look at the voting history of the United Nations we find that the veto power has not always been used to help those who are being oppressed or who are acting in the right way. In fact, we have seen that the veto power has, on certain occasions, been misused to help and assist in cruelty, rather than to prevent it. This is not something that is hidden or unknown; many commentators openly write or speak about this.

Another beautiful principle taught by Islam is that peace in society requires one to suppress his anger, rather than allowing it to prevail over principles of honesty and justice. The early history of Islam testifies that the true Muslims always acted upon this principle and those who did not were severely rebuked by the Holy Prophet Muhammad[sa]. Yet, today, unfortunately, this is not always the case. There are cases where armies or soldiers, who have been sent to establish peace, conduct themselves in a way that is entirely contrary to their stated aims. For example, in some countries foreign soldiers have treated the dead bodies of their victims in the most disrespectful and horrifying manner. Can peace be established in this way? The reaction to such behaviour cannot remain limited only to the affected country, but manifests throughout the world. Of course, if Muslims are mistreated, Muslim extremists take advantage of it and the peace of the world is shattered, although it is contrary to the teachings of Islam. Islam teaches that peace can only be established by helping both the oppressed and oppressor in a manner that is completely impartial, free from vested interests and devoid of all enmity. Peace is made by giving all parties an equal platform and playing field.

As the time is limited, I shall mention just one further point, which is that Islam teaches that the wealth and resources of others should not be looked upon enviously. We should not covet that which belongs to others, because this too is a means for peace to be dismantled. If wealthy countries try to extract and utilise the wealth and resources of less developed nations to fulfil their own needs, then naturally, restlessness will spread. Where appropriate, the developed nations can take a small and fair amount in return for their services, whilst the majority of resources should be utilised to help the under-developed countries to raise their standards of living. They should be allowed to prosper and should be helped in their efforts to reach the same levels as the developed world, because then, and only then can peace be established. If the leadership of those countries is not honest, then the Western nations or developed nations should themselves monitor and organise the development of the country by giving them aid.

There are numerous other points I could cover, but due to a lack of time, I shall restrict myself to the few that I have mentioned. Certainly, whatever I have explained represents the true teachings of Islam.

There is one question that may arise in your hearts and so let me address it in advance. You may say that if these are the true teachings of Islam, then why do we see such divisions and disorder in the Muslim world? This I have answered earlier by mentioning the need for the advent of a reformer, whom we believe was the Founder of the Ahmadiyya Muslim Community. We, the Ahmadiyya Muslim Jamā'at, always endeavour to convey these true teachings to as wide an audience as we can. I would request all of you to also make efforts to raise awareness within your own circles of influence about these issues, so that long lasting peace can be developed in all parts of the world.

If we fail in this task, then no part of the world will remain safe from the horrifying and destructive effects of war. I pray that may Allah the Almighty enable the people of the world to rise above their personal interests and desires, in an effort to save the world from the coming destruction. It is the developed nations of the West that hold the greatest amount of power in today's world, and so it is your duty, above others, to pay urgent attention to these matters of crucial importance.

At the end, I would like to once again thank all of you for taking the time to come and listen to what I have said. May Allah bless you.

Thank you very much.

CAN MUSLIMS INTEGRATE INTO WESTERN SOCIETIES?

BAITUR-RASHEED MOSQUE
HAMBURG, GERMANY, 2012

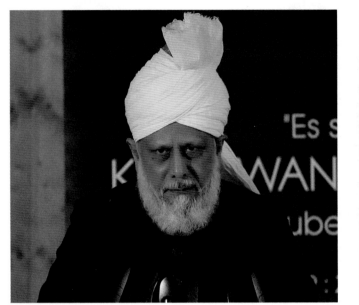

Ḥaḍrat Mirza Masroor Ahmad, Khalīfatul-Masīḥ V[aba]
delivers the keynote address at Baitur-Rasheed Mosque

Can Muslims Integrate Into Western Societies?

Bismillāhir-Raḥmānir-Raḥīm—In the name of Allah, the Gracious, Ever Merciful.

All distinguished guests—*assalāmo 'alaikum wa raḥmatullāhe wa barakātohū*—peace and blessings of Allah be upon you all.

First of all I would like to express my gratitude to all of the guests who have accepted our invitation to attend this event. Many of you are well-acquainted with our Community or have old ties of friendship with Ahmadi Muslims; and I am sure that those of you who have only recently been introduced to the Ahmadiyya Community will have already developed a keen desire in their hearts to learn more about the Jamā'at. The attendance of all of you proves that you believe that no danger or threat lies in meeting and keeping contact with Ahmadi Muslims and going to their mosques.

The truth is that in today's climate, where the majority of news and reports about Islam are extremely negative, those of you who are non-Muslims could easily have developed a concern that by visiting an Ahmadi Mosque it could lead to difficulties or even cause you a great deal of harm. However, as I said, the fact that you are attending this event proves you have no fear of Ahmadi Muslims and do not consider them to be a threat. It shows that you value Ahmadis and believe them to be sincere and decent people just like yourselves and the majority of the population.

Whilst saying this, I do not discount the possibility that there may be a small number of you who, in spite of coming today, still continue to harbour reservations or concerns that there could be some negative consequences of attending. It is possible you may be worried that you will be sat alongside people with extremist tendencies or mind-set. If any of you do hold such fears you should remove them from your hearts immediately. We are extremely vigilant in this regard and so if by chance any such extremist person tries to enter this mosque or our area, we will take firm action to remove them from the building. So be sure you are in safe hands.

Indeed, the Ahmadiyya Muslim Jamāʿat is a Community in which if any member at any time or place displays extremist tendencies, breaks the law or destroys the peace, they are expelled from the Jamāʿat (Community). We are duty bound to take such firm action because of our absolute respect for the word 'Islam' which literally means 'peace' and 'security'. The true representation of the word 'Islam' is demonstrated by our Community. The advent of this true depiction of Islam was actually foretold in a grand prophecy made by the Founder of Islam, the Holy Prophet Muhammad[sa], more than 1400 years ago. In the prophecy, the

Holy Prophet[sa] said that a time would come when the vast majority of Muslims would forget Islam's real and pure teachings. According to the prophecy, at such a time Allah would send one person as a Reformer, a Messiah and a Mahdi in order to re-establish true Islam in the world.

We, the Ahmadiyya Muslim Jamā'at, believe the Founder of our Community, Ḥaḍrat Mirza Ghulam Ahmad[as] of Qadian to be the very person sent in fulfilment of the great prophecy. With the Grace of Allah this Community has flourished and has spread to 202 countries of the world. In each of these countries, local people of all backgrounds and ethnicities have accepted Ahmadiyyat. Apart from being Ahmadi Muslims, they continue to play their roles as loyal citizens of their respective countries. There lies no contradiction or conflict between their love for Islam and their love for their country. In fact, both of these loyalties are intertwined and linked together. Ahmadi Muslims, wherever they reside, are the most law-abiding citizens in the entire nation. Certainly, I can say without a shadow of doubt that these qualities exist in a good majority of members of our Jamā'at.

It is due to these attributes that whenever Ahmadi Muslims migrate from one country to another, or in the case where local people have converted to Ahmadiyyat, the Ahmadis never have any concerns about integrating into their new societies; nor do they worry about how they will play their role towards furthering the wide scope of the national interests of their adopted nations. Wherever Ahmadis go they will love their countries like all true citizens should and will spend their lives actively seeking the betterment and progress of their nation. It is Islam that teaches us to live our lives in this way, and indeed it does not just gently advocate this, but actually commands us to be absolutely loyal and devoted to our country of residence. Indeed, the Holy Prophet[sa] particularly emphasised that love for one's nation is a part of faith for any true Muslim. When loving your country is a basic element of Islam, how can any true Muslim exhibit disloyalty or betray his nation and thereby forgo his faith? In terms of Ahmadi Muslims, at our major events all members of the Community, whether they are men, women, children or the elderly, stand up and make a pledge taking God as their witness. In that pledge they promise to give up their lives, wealth, time and honour not just for their religion but also for the sake of their nations and countries. Therefore, who could prove to be more loyal citizens than those people who are constantly reminded to serve their nation and from whom a pledge is repeatedly taken to be ever-ready to make all sacrifices for the sake of their faith, country and nation?

The question may arise in the minds of some people that here in Germany, the majority of Muslims come from Pakistan, Turkey or other Asian countries, and so when the time comes to make sacrifices for their nations, they will prefer their countries of origin, rather than Germany. Thus, I should clarify and explain that when a person acquires German nationality or the nationality of any country, then he becomes a full citizen of that nation. I made this very point earlier this year when I delivered an address at the German Military Headquarters, in Koblenz. I explained, according to Islamic teachings, what should happen if a situation arises whereby Germany is engaged in a war with the country of origin of an immigrant who has become a German citizen. If the immigrant feels sympathy towards his original country and thinks there is a risk of him desiring or causing harm to Germany, then such a person should immediately relinquish his citizenship or immigration status and return to his native country. However, if he chooses to remain, then Islam does not permit any form of disloyalty to the country whatsoever. This is an absolute and unequivocal teaching. Islam does not permit any form of rebellious behaviour, or for a citizen to scheme against his nation—whether adopted nation or otherwise—or to harm it any way. If a person does work against his adopted nation or causes it harm then he should be treated as an enemy of the state, a traitor and be punished according to the laws of the land.

That clarifies the situation in terms of a Muslim immigrant. In the case where a local German or a person of any country, who has converted to Islam, it is perfectly clear that for him or her, there can be no other path than to display absolute loyalty to his or her great nation. Another question sometimes asked is: what action should Muslims who live in the West take when a Western country engages in war with a Muslim nation? To answer this I should first of all mention that the Founder of our Community, the Promised Messiah[as], has explained that we are now in an era where religious wars have completely come to an end. During the course of history there were times when wars and battles took place between Muslims and the people of other religions. During those battles the goal of the non-Muslims was to kill the Muslims and end Islam.

In most of the early wars, the non-Muslims took the first aggressive steps and so the Muslims had no choice but to defend themselves and their religion. However, the Promised Messiah[as] explained that such circumstances no longer exist, because there are no modern day governments who are declaring or waging war in an effort to end Islam. To the contrary, there is a great deal of religious freedom in the vast majority of Western and non-Muslim countries. Our Jamāʿat is extremely grateful that such freedoms exist, which allow Ahmadi Muslims to propagate the message of Islam in non-Muslim countries. Therefore we are able to introduce the real and beautiful teachings of Islam, which are of peace and harmony, to the Western world. Certainly, it is due to religious freedom and tolerance that I am able to stand before you today and present the true Islam. Clearly therefore, today there is no question of religious wars. The only other situation that can arise is where a majority Muslim country and a majority Christian country, or any other country, are engaged in a non-religious war. How should a Muslim citizen living in those countries, whether Christian or any other religion, react to such circumstances? To answer this question, Islam has provided a golden principle, which is that a person should never assist in cruelty or oppression. Therefore, if cruelty or oppression is perpetrated by a Muslim country then it should be stopped. If cruelty is conducted by a Christian country then that too should be stopped.

How can an individual citizen stop his own country from cruelty and injustice? The answer to this is very simple. In the present day, democracy is prevalent throughout the Western world. If a just minded citizen sees that his government is acting in an oppressive way, then he should raise his voice in opposition and seek to guide his country to the right path—or even a group of people can rise up. If a citizen sees that his country is violating the sovereignty of another nation, then he should draw the attention of his government and raise his concerns. To stand up and peacefully lodge your concerns is not an act of rebellion or revolt. In fact, it is an expression of true love for your country. A just citizen cannot bear to see the reputation of his country being tarnished or even disgraced amongst the international community and so by calling his country to account he is manifesting his love and loyalty towards it.

As far as the international community and its institutions are concerned, Islam teaches that where a country is unjustly attacked, other nations should unite and seek to stop the aggressor. If the aggressive nation comes to its senses and withdraws, then cruel punishments and unjust decisions should not be imposed upon it in revenge or as a means to take advantage of the situation. Therefore, Islam provides the answers and remedies to all possible situations. The essence of Islamic teachings is that you must spread peace, to the extent that the Holy Prophet[sa] has defined a Muslim as a person from whose hand and tongue all other peaceful people are safe. As I have already said, Islam has taught that you must never assist in cruelty or oppression. It is this beautiful and wise teaching that leads a true Muslim to hold a position of honour and dignity within whichever country he lives. There is no doubt that all sincere and decent people would wish to have such peaceful and considerate people within their societies.

The Holy Prophet Muhammad[sa] has given Muslims another beautiful teaching to live their lives by. He taught that a true believer should always search for anything that is good and pure. He taught that wherever a Muslim comes across a word of wisdom or anything noble, he should treat it as his personal inheritance. Thus, with the same determination that a person seeks to acquire his rightful inheritance, Muslims are taught they should strive to obtain and benefit from wise counsel and goodness wherever it may be found. At a time when there are so many concerns about the integration of immigrants, what a beautiful and perfect guiding principle this is. Muslims have been taught that in order to integrate with their local societies and develop mutual respect, they should seek to learn about all of the good aspects of every society, every region, every city and every country. It is not enough to simply learn about such values, but Muslims must endeavour to adopt them into their own personal lives. This is guidance that truly inculcates togetherness and a spirit of mutual trust and love. Indeed, who can be more peace loving than a true believer, who apart from fulfilling the requirements of his faith, also tries to adopt all of the good aspects of his or any other society? Who can spread peace and security more than him?

Due to the means of communication available today, the world is now known as a global village. This was something that the Holy Prophet[sa] prophesised about 1400 years ago when he said that a time would come when the world would become like one and distances would appear to shorten. He said that due to the fast and modern means of communication, people would be able to see the entire world. In fact, this is a prophecy of the Holy Qur'an, which he explained at length. Regarding this, the Holy Prophet[sa] taught that when such a time comes, people should seek to learn and embrace the good things of one another, in the same way that they would seek to find their lost property. In other words, it can be said that all positive things should be adopted, whilst all negative things should be shunned. The Holy Qur'an has explained this commandment by saying a true Muslim is he who enjoins good and forbids evil. Bearing all of this in mind, which country or society can say that it cannot tolerate or accept for such peace loving Muslims or Islam to be amongst them? Last year I had the opportunity to meet the Mayor of Berlin and I explained to him that Islam teaches that you should treat every good aspect of any nation as though it was your own personal property. In response, he said, that if you act upon this teaching then there is no doubt the entire world will join hands and support you.

I am quite astonished and saddened when I hear that in some parts of Germany there are people who claim that neither Muslims nor Islam have the capability to integrate into German society. Certainly, it is true that the Islam presented by extremists or terrorists does not have the ability to integrate with any country or society, let alone just Germany. Indeed, a time will surely come when voices of opposition to such extremist ideologies will be raised loudly even in Muslim countries. Nonetheless, the true Islam, which was brought by the Holy Prophet[sa], will certainly always attract sincere and decent people towards it. In this era, to revive the original teachings, Allah sent the Promised Messiah[as] in servitude to the Holy Prophet[sa] and so his Community practices and preaches the true message of Islam.

Let it be clear that no one can justifiably claim that true Islam cannot integrate into any society. True Islam is that which spreads righteousness and goodness and shuns all forms of evil and wrongdoing. True Islam teaches Muslims to stop evil and cruelty wherever it exists. Thus, rather than any question of it failing to integrate, true Islam naturally pulls society towards it like a magnet. Islam teaches that a person should not just strive to acquire or desire peace for himself, but should make full efforts to spread peace and harmony to other people with the same longing they hold for themselves. This selfless attitude is the way to establish peace in the world. Is there any society that would not appreciate such teachings and would not approve of such an approach? Certainly, a good society could never desire immorality and evil to be spread within it, and it would never oppose for goodness and peace to be promoted.

When we come to define 'goodness', it is possible that there may be differences in defining it between a religious person and a non-religious person. Amongst the aspects of goodness and virtue that Islam speaks of, there are two overarching virtues, through which all other forms of goodness emanate. One is the right due to Allah the Almighty and the other is the right due to mankind. Whilst there is a difference in definition in terms of one aspect between a religious person and a non-religious person, in terms of the other aspect, that is the right of mankind, there is none. The rights due to Allah relate to worship and all religions guide their followers with regard to this. In terms of the rights due to man, these are something that both religions and societies have educated mankind about. Islam teaches us in great depth and detail about the rights of mankind and so to cover all of its teachings at this time would prove to be impossible. However, I will mention a few of the important rights established by Islam, which are necessary for peace to develop within society.

Islam teaches you must respect and care for the sentiments of other people. This includes religious sentiments and the feelings of others in relation to general social issues. On one occasion, in order to safeguard the religious sensitivities of a Jewish man, the Holy Prophet[sa] sided with the Jew after he reported an argument that had taken place between him and a Muslim. To spare the feelings of the Jewish person, the Holy Prophet[sa] rebuked the Muslim by saying that he should not claim that the Holy Prophet[sa] was superior to Moses, although he knew that he had brought the final Law-Bearing Book. This is the manner in which the Holy Prophet[sa] took care of the feelings of others and established peace within society.

Another great teaching of Islam requires for the rights of the poor and deprived people to be fulfilled. In order to do this, it teaches that people should search for opportunities through which the social standing of the deprived segments of society can be improved. We should seek to help the disadvantaged in a selfless manner and should never exploit them in any way. Unfortunately, in today's society where projects or opportunities are created to apparently 'help' the disadvantaged, they are often based on a system of credit where the repayment is subject to interest. For example, students are often given loans to help them complete their education or people take loans to start businesses, yet it takes them years or even decades to repay them. If after years of struggle, or an economic crisis strikes, then they can end up at the original level of debt or quite possibly in an even worse financial state. We have witnessed or heard about countless examples of this during the past few years, when many parts of the world have been plagued by a financial crisis.

An allegation commonly made against Islam is that it does not treat women in a fair or equal way. However, this allegation is without any foundation or basis. Islam has given women dignity and honour; I give one or two examples. Islam gave a woman the right to divorce her husband due to wrong behaviour, at a time when women were considered merely a possession or chattel. It is only in the past century that in the developed world this right has been properly established for women. Furthermore, Islam gave women the right to inherit at a time when women were deemed to have no status or worth. This right has also only been granted to the women of Europe in relatively recent times. Islam also imparts a right to one's neighbours.

The Qur'an gives detailed guidance about who constitutes your neighbour and what their rights are. Neighbours include those who sit next to you, the houses nearby, including those who you know and even those who you do not know and, in fact, it encompasses the forty houses surrounding you. Also included as your neighbours are those with whom you travel and so we are commanded to take care of them. This right was emphasised so much that the Holy Prophet[sa] said he thought that perhaps neighbours would be included amongst the prescribed heirs. In fact, the Holy Prophet[sa] went as far as to say that a person from whom his neighbour is not safe cannot be classed as a believer or a Muslim.

Another commandment of Islam for the well-being of others requires all parties to help and support one another in fulfilling the duty to help the weak and vulnerable rise and improve their status. Thus, in order to fulfil its role and to implement these teachings, the Ahmadiyya Muslim Jamā'at is providing primary and higher education in poor and deprived parts of the world. We are building and running schools, providing stipends and funding scholarships for higher education so that those who are deprived can get to a position where they are able to stand upon their own two feet.

Another commandment of Islam is that you must fulfil all of your pledges and covenants. This includes all promises that you make with one another and also requires that a Muslim must fulfil the pledge of loyalty that he makes to his country as a citizen. This is something that I spoke about earlier.

These are just a few points I have mentioned to demonstrate to you the extent to which Islam is such a compassionate and loving religion. It is a matter of great sadness that with the same force that Islam teaches and counsels peace in the world, the opponents of Islam or those who are unacquainted with its true teachings, are raising unfounded allegations against it. As I have said, in this era, the Ahmadiyya Muslim Jamāʿat is propagating and displaying the true message of Islam. In light of this I would request those who raise objections against Islam on the basis of the actions of a minority of Muslims, to certainly question and hold to account those individuals, but they should not use such unjust examples to defame and discredit the true teachings of Islam.

You should not consider the teachings of Islam to be dangerous or a threat to Germany or to any other country. You should not be concerned about whether or not a Muslim can integrate into German society. As I have already said, a distinction of Islam is that it teaches Muslims to adopt all good things and so there is no doubt that Muslims can integrate and live within any society. If somebody does something contrary to it, he is a Muslim by name, but not the follower of the true teachings of Islam. Certainly, if Muslims are asked to do something that is not right or are told to disregard the instructions of the Holy Qur'an relating to the principles of modesty, the sanctity of the religion or to act against righteousness, then they cannot do so. However, such matters are not a question of integration, but are actually about personal religious freedom.

The violation of religious freedom is not only a question for

Muslims alone to stand up against, but in fact all sincere and decent people stand up and speak against this and openly declare that no government or society should interfere with personal religious rights. It is my prayer that Germany, and indeed every country that has become a home to people of different nationalities and cultures, display the highest standards of tolerance and respect for each other's feelings and sentiments. In this way, may they become standard bearers for those who display mutual love, affection and peace. This will be the means for guaranteeing the world's permanent peace and security, so the world can be saved from the destruction that it is heading towards as a result of a complete lack of mutual tolerance.

The threat of horrific destruction is looming over us and so to save us from such devastation, every country and every individual, whether religious or not, needs to tread very, very carefully. May every person throughout the world come to realise this reality. At the end I would like to once again thank all of you for taking the time to come and attend and listen to what I have said today. May Allah bless you all.

Thank you very much.

ISLAM—
RELIGION OF PEACE AND COMPASSION

HOUSES OF PARLIAMENT
LONDON, UK, 2013

The Deputy Prime Minister, Rt. Hon. Nick Clegg in discussion with Ḥaḍrat Khalifatul-Masiḥ V[aba], House of Commons, London, 11th June 2013

The Home Secretary, Rt. Hon. Theresa May MP with Ḥaḍrat Khalifatul-Masiḥ V[aba]

The Shadow Foreign Minister Rt. Hon. Douglas Alexander with Ḥaḍrat Khalifatul-Masiḥ V[aba]

Rt. Hon. Ed Davey MP with Ḥaḍrat Khalifatul-Masiḥ V[aba]

Ḥaḍrat Khalifatul-Masiḥ V[aba] received at the House of Commons by Rt. Hon. Ed Davey MP London, 11th June 2013

Rt. Hon. Ed Davey MP escorts Ḥaḍrat Khalifatul-Masiḥ V[aba] through Westminster Hall, House of Commons, London, 11th June 2013

Ḥaḍrat Khalifatul-Masiḥ V[aba] delivering his historic speech to Parliamentarians, VIPs and diplomats at the House of Commons, London, 11th June 2013

Preface

On 11th June 2013, His Holiness, Mirza Masroor Ahmad, Khalīfatul-Masīḥ V[aba] (may Allah be his helper), Head of the worldwide Ahmadiyya Muslim Community delivered an address at an event to celebrate the centenary of the Ahmadiyya Muslim Community in the United Kingdom, held at the Houses of Parliament in London.

The centenary celebrations were attended by 68 dignitaries, including 30 MPs and 12 Members of the House of Lords, including 6 Cabinet Ministers and 2 Ministers. Various media organisations including the BBC, Sky TV and ITV were also present to cover the event. In attendance, amongst others, was the Secretary of State for Energy and Climate Change The Rt. Hon. Ed Davey MP, the Deputy Prime Minister The Rt. Hon. Nick Clegg MP, the Home Secretary The Rt. Hon. Theresa May MP, the Shadow Foreign Secretary The Rt. Hon. Douglas Alexander MP, the Chairman of the Home Affairs Select Committee Rt. Hon. Keith

Vaz MP and Member of Parliament for Mitcham and Morden
Siobhain McDonaugh MP.

Islam—
A Religion of Peace and Compassion

Bismillāhir-Raḥmānir-Raḥīm—In the name of Allah, the Gracious, Ever Merciful.

All distinguished guests—*assalāmo 'alaikum wa raḥmatullāhe wa barakātohū*—peace and blessings of Allah be upon you all.

First of all I would like to thank those friends of the Ahmadiyya Muslim Community who, upon the centenary of our Community in the UK, have kindly organised this event within the Houses of Parliament as a means to express their friendship and close relationship with us. I would also like to thank all of those guests, who by attending today, are ensuring that this event proves to be a success and worthwhile. I am pleased that quite a number of you are seated here and are not engaged in any other commitments or meetings.

In response to this gesture, apart from professing my thanks and appreciation, I would also like to say that it is my sincere hope and prayer that all of the departments and people who work within this beautiful and grand building are able to fulfil the rights of serving this country and its people. I also hope and pray that they are able to work in the best possible manner towards fostering good relations with other nations, to act with justice and so make decisions that are of benefit to all parties. If this spirit is adopted then it will reap the very best fruits, which are of love, affection and brotherhood and will lead the world towards becoming a true haven of peace and prosperity.

This desire and prayer of mine is shared by all Ahmadi Muslims, because we believe that it is necessary to have a deep love for one's country and for humanity at large. Indeed, Ahmadi Muslims believe that love for one's country is an essential part of faith, because the Founder of Islam, the Holy Prophet Muhammad[sa] has emphatically ordered and taught this. Thus, let me make it very clear that every Ahmadi Muslim who is a British citizen, whether born here in the UK or whether an immigrant from abroad, is completely loyal to this country and has sincere love for it. They desire only the progress and prosperity of this great nation.

The number of people from other nations who now live in the UK is very significant and is estimated to be at around 14-15% of the total population of this country. And so, I cannot continue without mentioning and praising the great qualities of openheartedness and tolerance exhibited by the local British people, for the way in which they have accepted immigrants as members of the country and allowed them to become a part of the fabric of British society. In this sense it becomes an incumbent moral duty upon those people who have come to settle here to prove themselves to be loyal citizens of this country and so they must support the government in its efforts to tackle all forms of disorder and strife. As far as the Ahmadiyya Muslim Community is concerned, its members act upon this principle in whichever country they reside.

As you are aware, we are currently celebrating the Centenary of the Ahmadiyya Muslim Jamāʻat in the United Kingdom. These past 100 years prove and serve witness to the fact that the members of the Ahmadiyya Community have always fulfilled the requirement of being loyal to their country and have always steered absolutely clear of all forms of extremism, rebellion and disorder. In reality, the fundamental reason for this loyal and loving approach is due entirely to the fact that the Ahmadiyya Muslim Community is a true Islamic religious community. Our Community stands apart, as we have continually introduced the true and peaceful teachings of Islam to the people of the world and we have always strived for those true teachings to become accepted as the real Islam.

With these few words of introduction, I would now like to turn towards the main theme of my address. Our sect is the standard bearer for peace, reconciliation and harmony, which is why our motto is 'Love for All, Hatred for None.' Despite the fact that some non-Muslims know us or indeed have close links to us, they are very surprised that the Ahmadiyya Muslim Jamāʻat attributes its message of peace and brotherhood directly to Islam. The cause of their surprise and shock is because they see that many other so-called Islamic scholars and organisations act and speak in a completely different way and promote a very different message. To explain this difference let me make it clear that we Ahmadi

Muslims believe that, in this era, the concept of a violent 'Jihad by the sword' is completely wrong and is to be rejected, whilst some other Muslim scholars promote or even practice it. Their beliefs have led to many extremist and terrorist organisations emerging amongst the Muslims in various parts of the world.

It is not just groups that are emerging but we also find that certain individuals are taking advantage of and acting upon these false beliefs. The most recent example of this was, of course, the brutal killing of an innocent British soldier on the streets of London. It was an attack which had absolutely nothing to do with the real teachings of Islam; rather, Islamic teachings vehemently condemn such acts. Such evil plots demonstrate the clear difference between the true teachings of Islam and the misconstrued teachings, which some so-called Muslims are practicing due to their ulterior motives. I would also like to say that the reaction of some of the local groups is not correct and can destroy the peace of the society.

What evidence is there to support our contention that what we believe with regards to Islamic teachings is correct? The underlying point to consider is that the use of the sword or force is only permissible when a religious war is waged against Islam. In today's world no one, be it a country or a religion, is physically waging war and attacking Islam on the basis of religion. Thus, it is not justifiable in any way for Muslims to attack any other party, in the name of religion, because this clearly violates the teachings of the Qur'an.

The Qur'an only permitted force to be used against those who waged war and raised their sword against Islam. Another crucial point is that if a citizen seeks to inflict any form of harm on his country or on his fellow countrymen then clearly he would be acting against the teachings of Islam. The Holy Prophet Muhammad[sa] said that whoso sheds the blood of an innocent person is not a Muslim. The Holy Prophet[sa] has deemed such people as weak in faith and to be sinners.

I shall now turn to some other aspects of Islam that prove just how enlightened and pure its teachings really are. I shall explain that the way some so-called Muslim groups present Islam does not represent the real teachings of the religion in any shape or form. It will become clear that their activities are conducted with the sole desire to fulfil their vested interests by falsely using the name of Islam to justify their hate-filled acts.

Islam puts so much emphasis on the importance of religious tolerance that it will be impossible to find such high standards anywhere else. Other people tend to believe that until other religions are proven to be false, they are unable to prove the truth of their religion. Islam's approach is very different because it teaches that whilst Islam is a true religion sent for all of mankind, the truth is that all prophets of God were sent to all people and nations of the world. This is clearly mentioned in the Holy Qur'an. Allah has said that all prophets were sent by Him with teachings of love and affection, and so all true Muslims must accept them. No other religion so willingly and openly praises every faith and every nation as Islam does. Because Muslims believe that prophets were sent to all people and all nations they cannot ever consider them to be false. Thus, Muslims cannot disrespect, mock or insult any of the prophets of God, nor can they injure the sentiments of the followers of any religion.

Yet, sadly the attitude of some non-Muslims is the exact

opposite. They do not spare any opportunity to grievously mock and slander the Founder of Islam[sa] and so gravely wound the feelings of Muslims. We truly desire religious tolerance and mutual understanding, because of the beliefs we hold. Unfortunately however, when certain elements toy with the feelings of Muslims, it leads to some so-called Muslims reacting to the provocation in an entirely wrong and irresponsible way. Their reaction and response has no link to the true teachings of Islam and you will certainly find that no Ahmadi Muslim, however much they are provoked, will ever react in such a negative manner.

Another grave allegation raised against the Founder of Islam[sa] and the Qur'an is that they gave teachings of extremism and promoted the use of force to spread the message of Islam. To assess this allegation and to seek the reality let us look to the Qur'an itself. Allah the Almighty says:

And if thy Lord had *enforced* His Will, surely, all who are in the earth would have believed together. Wilt thou, then, force men to become believers? (ch. 10: v. 100)

This verse clearly states that God, as the Possessor of all Powers, could easily force all people to adopt the same religion; however, He has instead given the people of the world the freedom to choose - to believe or to not believe.

And so if God has given mankind this freedom of choice, then how could the Holy Prophet Muhammad[sa] or any of his followers compel or force anyone to become a Muslim? Allah the Almighty also states in the Qur'an:

...It is the truth from your Lord; wherefore let him who will believe, and let him, who will disbelieve... (ch. 18: v.30)

This is the reality of Islam. This is its true teaching. If a person's heart desires then they are free to accept Islam, but if their heart does not, then they are free to reject it. Therefore, Islam is completely against compulsion and extremism; rather, it advocates peace and harmony at all levels of society. It is quite impossible for Islam to teach violence or compulsion because the very meaning of 'Islam' is to live in peace and to provide peace to all others. Nevertheless, when our religious sentiments are taunted it causes us great pain and anguish. Anything disrespectful said about the Holy Prophet Muhammad[sa] pierces and wounds our hearts.

It was the Founder of Islam[sa] who developed the love of God and the love of His creation in our hearts. It was he who ingrained and established love and respect for all of mankind and for all religions within us. What bigger proof of Islam's peaceful teachings can there be than the response given by the opponents of the Holy Prophet[sa] when he preached and conveyed the message of Islam to them. They did not say that by inviting them to join Islam, the Holy Prophet[sa] was asking them to perpetrate any cruelties or wrongdoing. Rather, their reply was that if they were to accept the Prophet's teachings, their wealth and status would be threatened or seized by ruthless people, because the Holy Prophet[sa] emphasised only peace and harmony. They admitted to a fear that if they accepted Islam then by adopting peace the surrounding people, tribes or even nations would take advantage and destroy them. In short, if Islam advocated violence, and if it called on Muslims to raise their swords and wage war, then clearly the disbelievers would not have given this justification. They would not have said that their failure to accept Islam was out of a fear that its teachings of peace could lead to their ruin at the hands of worldly people.

The Holy Qur'an states that one of the Attributes of God Almighty is *Salam* which means He is 'The Source of Peace.' It follows that if God truly is the 'Source of Peace' then His peace should encompass all of His Creation and all of mankind, rather than be limited to a specific group of people. If God's peace was only designed to protect some people then it cannot be said that He is a God for the entire world. Allah the Almighty has answered this point in the Qur'an. Allah says:

> I *swear* by his *repeated* cry "O my Lord!" that these are a people who will not believe. Therefore, turn aside from them, and say, "Peace;" and soon shall they know. (ch. 43: v. 89-90)

These words illustrate that the Holy Prophet Muhammad[sa] brought a teaching that was a source of mercy and compassion for all people and thus was a means of peace for all of mankind. The verse also states that in response to the Holy Prophet's[sa] message of peace, his opponents did not only reject his teachings; they even ridiculed and insulted him. Indeed, they went even further and opposed him with enmity and created disorder and strife. Upon all of this the Holy Prophet[sa] pleaded to God that *I desire to give them peace, but they do not give me peace. Leaving that aside they even strive to inflict pain and agony upon me.*

In response, Allah consoled him by saying that *ignore whatever they do and turn away from them. Your only task is to spread and establish peace in the world. You should respond to their hatred and transgressions by simply saying "peace be with you" and tell them that you have brought peace for them.*

Thus, the Holy Prophet[sa] spent his entire life spreading peace in the world. That was his noble mission. Certainly, there will come a day when the people of the world will realise and understand that he did not bring any teachings of extremism. They will realise that all he brought was a message of peace, love and kindness. Furthermore, if the followers of this noble messenger also respond to cruelties and injustices in the same loving manner, then no doubt those who raise objections against Islam's magnificent teachings will one day become convinced of its truth and beauty.

The Ahmadiyya Muslim Jamāʿat follows and lives by these teachings. It is these teachings of understanding, tolerance and compassion that we promote and spread to the corners of the world. We follow the historic and unparalleled example of kindness and benevolence that was demonstrated by the Holy Prophet Muhammad[sa] when after years of facing the most bitter and horrific cruelty and persecution, he was able to return victoriously to the streets of Makkah. For years, he and his followers, were prevented access to even the most basic necessities such as food and water and so they spent many days at a time suffering in a state of starvation. Many of his followers were attacked and some were killed in the most barbaric and merciless manner, which one cannot even imagine. Even the elderly Muslims, the Muslim women and the Muslim children were not spared; rather, they too were treated in a ruthless and brutal way. Yet, when the Holy Prophet[sa] returned to Makkah in victory, he did not seek revenge.

Instead, he proclaimed that *there shall be no punishment upon any of you for I have forgiven you all. I am a messenger of love and peace. I have the greatest knowledge of Allah's attribute of being a 'Source of Peace' – He is the One Who gives peace. Thus, I forgive you of all of your past transgressions and I give you a guarantee of peace and security. You are free to remain in Makkah and to freely practise your religion. No one will be compelled or forced in any way.*

Some of the most staunch disbelievers had fled Makkah in a state of fear of punishment because they knew they had exceeded all limits in their cruelties against the Muslims. However, upon witnessing this unrivalled act of compassion and kindness and this unique display of peace and harmony, the relatives of those disbelievers sent a message to them to return. They were informed that the Holy Prophet[sa] extended nothing but peace and security and so they did return to Makkah. When they, who were previously Islam's most resolute opponents, saw for themselves the benevolence and mercy of the Holy Prophet[sa], they accepted Islam of their own free will.

What I have said is part of recorded history and the majority of non-Muslim historians and Orientalists have also certified to its truth. These are the real teachings of Islam and this was the noble example of the Holy Prophet Muhammad[sa]. And so to label Islam and its Founder as violent and to raise such allegations against them is a cruel injustice. There is no doubt that wherever such false allegations are made we are deeply aggrieved.

I shall say again that today it is our community, the Ahmadiyya Muslim Jamā'at, which is following and living according to the original and peaceful teachings of Islam.

And I shall say again that the hate-filled evil acts perpetrated by extremist organisations or individuals have no link whatsoever to the true teachings of Islam.

True justice requires that the vested interests of individuals or groups should not be attributed to the teachings of a religion. Such acts should not be used as an excuse to unfairly level criticism at any religion or its founder. It is an urgent need of the time that, in an effort to establish global peace and harmony, all people should display mutual respect for one another and for all religions. The alternatives are horrific.

The world has become a global village and so a lack of mutual respect and a failure to join together to promote peace will not only harm the local area, city or country but in fact will ultimately lead to the destruction of the entire world. We are all well-aware of the horrific devastation caused by the last two world wars. Due to the acts of certain countries the signs are that another world war is on the horizon.

If a world war breaks out then the Western world will also be deeply affected by its far-reaching and devastating consequences. Let us save ourselves from such destruction. Let us save our future generations from the miserable and devastating consequences of war. Obviously the most horrific type of war would be an atomic war and certainly the way the world is heading there is a real risk of a nuclear war breaking out. To prevent such a horrific outcome, we should adopt justice, integrity and honesty and join together to suppress and stop those groups who wish to spread hatred and who wish to destroy the peace of the world.

It is my hope and prayer that God Almighty enables the major powers to discharge their responsibilities and duties in this effort in the most fair and just way—*Amin.*

Before concluding I would like to once again thank all of you for taking the time and effort to attend today. May Allah bless you all.

Thank you very much.

WORLD PEACE—
THE CRITICAL NEED OF THE TIME

NEW ZEALAND NATIONAL PARLIAMENT
WELLINGTON , NEW ZEALAND, 2013

Hon. Kanwaljit Singh Bakshi (MP) receiving the Holy Qur'an from Ḥaḍrat Khalifatul-Masiḥ V[aba]

Iranian ambassador Seyed Majid Tafreshi Khameneh meeting Ḥaḍrat Khalifatul-Masiḥ V[aba]

Det. Rakesh Naidoo meeting Ḥaḍrat Khalifatul-Masiḥ V[aba] in representation of the Commissioner of Police New Zealand

Ḥaḍrat Khalifatul-Masiḥ V[aba] leading silent prayers at the conclusion of the official function in the Grand Hall, New Zealand Parliament

Dr. Cam Calder MP meeting Ḥaḍrat Khalifatul-Masiḥ V[aba]

Hadrat Khalifatul-Masih V[aba] delivering the
keynote address at the Grand Hall, in the
New Zealand Parliament. 4th Nov 2013

Hon. Kanwaljit Singh Bakshi (MP) with Hadrat Khalifatul-Masih V[aba]
and his entourage in front of the New Zealand Parliament

Preface

The worldwide Head of the Ahmadiyya Muslim Community, Ḥaḍrat Mirza Masroor Ahmad[aba], Khalīfatul-Masīḥ V, delivered an historic address at New Zealand's National Parliament in Wellington on 4th November 2013. In front of an audience of parliamentarians, ambassadors of state, academics and a range of other guests, the *Khalīfah*[aba] of the Promised Messiah[as] advocated the urgent need for justice as a means to develop world peace in the face of increasing tensions and conflicts in various parts of the world. After the keynote address, other dignitaries also addressed the event. Kanwaljit Singh Bakshi, MP, said: "It is our privilege to have His Holiness Ḥaḍrat Mirza Masroor Ahmad here in New Zealand's Parliament and to listen to have his wisdom and to listen to his thoughts." Dr. Rajen Prasad, MP, said: "It is a pleasure to welcome His Holiness to the New Zealand Parliament. I have always been very impressed at how Ahmadis live their lives as citizens of the nation and practice their message of peace." Upon the conclusion of the event, Ḥaḍrat Mirza Masroor Ahmad[aba] met with various dignitaries including the Ambassadors of Iran and Israel. His Holiness was then given a tour of Parliament by Kanwaljit Singh Bakshi MP.

World Peace—
The Critical Need of the Time

Bismillāhir-Raḥmānir-Raḥīm—In the name of Allah, the Gracious, Ever Merciful.

All distinguished guests—*assalāmo ʿalaikum wa raḥmatullāhe wa barakātohū*—peace and blessings of Allah be upon you all.

First of all I would like to take this opportunity to thank all of those people who have organised this event, in particular the honourable Member of Parliament, Kanwaljit Singh Bakshi, and have given me the opportunity to address all of you today. Secondly, I would like to thank all of you who have come here to listen to me.

Of course, in this Parliament House, the various politicians and members of parliament regularly meet to develop policies and plans and to enact legislation all aimed at making the nation progress. Apart from this, I am sure many secular or worldly leaders will have come here and addressed you based on their knowledge, expertise and past experiences. However rarely, if ever, will you have been addressed by the head of a religious community and in particular a Muslim leader. Thus, for you to give me the opportunity to address you, as the worldwide Head of the Ahmadiyya Muslim Community, which is a purely Islamic organisation and whose sole objective is to spread the true teachings of Islam, is a sign of your open-heartedness and your very high levels of tolerance. Therefore, I am obliged to thank you for this kind gesture.

With these words of thanks, I would now like to move on to the main part of my address and say a few things about Islam's beautiful teachings. I will speak about that issue, which in my opinion is the critical need of the time - and that is the establishment of world peace. From a secular perspective many of you, both politicians at an individual level and the government collectively, are making efforts towards achieving peace. Your efforts will be motivated by a good intent and you will have enjoyed some success in these efforts. Also, over the years, your government will have given advice to other major powers about the means to develop a peaceful and harmonious world.

No doubt, the state and circumstances of the world today are extremely precarious and are causing a great deal of concern to the entire world. Whilst some of the major conflicts today are taking place in the Arab world, the truth is that any wise or intelligent person will be aware that such conflicts will not remain limited to just that region. There is no doubt that a conflict between a government and its people can escalate into a much broader international conflict. Already, we find that two blocs amongst the major powers are forming. One bloc supports the Syrian Government, whilst the other is supporting the rebel forces. And so clearly this situation is not merely a grave threat to the Muslim countries but is also a source of extreme danger for the rest of the world.

We should never forget the heart-wrenching experiences of the two World Wars that occurred during the last century. The sheer devastation that they caused, in particular the Second World War, was unprecedented. Just through the use of conventional weapons heavily populated and thriving towns and cities were utterly demolished and left in absolute ruin and millions were killed. Further, during the Second World War the world witnessed that truly devastating event when the atom bomb was used against Japan causing such annihilation that just hearing of its effects makes a person tremble and shudder. The museums in Hiroshima and Nagasaki are a sufficient reminder of the horrors and utter devastation that took place.

During the Second World War around 70 million people were killed and it is said that 40 million of those who died were civilians. Thus more civilians sacrificed their lives than military personnel. Further, the aftermath of the war was truly terrifying, whereby the post-war related deaths ran into millions. For many years after the nuclear bombs were used, radiation continued to have a terrible degenerative effect on new-born children. In today's world, even some small nations have come to possess nuclear weapons and their leaders are trigger happy. It seems they do not care about the destructive consequences of their actions.

And so if we imagine a nuclear war occurring today, the picture painted leaves a person shaken and utterly petrified. The atom bombs possessed by smaller nations today are perhaps even more powerful than those that were used during the Second World War. And so this climate of conflict and instability can only cause great concern to those people who wish to establish peace in the world and who are working towards it.

The pathetic situation of today's world is that at one level, people speak of establishing peace, whilst at another level they are engulfed in their egotistical ways and wrapped by a shroud of pride and arrogance. In order to prove their superiority and might, every powerful government is ready to make all possible efforts. After the Second World War, in an effort to establish long-lasting peace in the world and to prevent future wars, nations joined together to form an organisation, which they called the United Nations. However, it seems that just as the League of Nations miserably failed in its objectives, the status and respect of the United Nations continues to fall by the day. If the requirements of justice are not fulfilled, then no matter how many organisations are formed for the sake of peace, their efforts will prove fruitless.

I have just mentioned the failure of the League of Nations. The institution was formed after the First World War, with the sole objective of safeguarding world peace; however it could not stop the onset of the Second World War, which as I have already said caused so much devastation and loss. New Zealand also suffered casualties as a result of the war. It is said that it suffered a loss of around 11,000 people, virtually all of whom were from the military. As New Zealand was far removed from the epicentre of the war it did not suffer civilian casualties. However, as I have already alluded to, overall in the war more innocent civilians were killed than military personnel. Just imagine: normal innocent people, including countless women and children, were killed indiscriminately having committed no crime.

It is for this very reason that you will find in the hearts of people who live in countries which were directly engulfed in that war an innate hatred of war itself. Certainly, it is a requirement of loving one's nation that if it is ever attacked, it is the duty of a citizen to be ready to give every sacrifice for its defence and to liberate the nation. Nevertheless, if the conflict can be resolved in a cordial or peaceful way through negotiations and diplomacy then one should not needlessly invite death and killings. In olden times when wars took place, there were mainly military casualties with a very minimum civilian loss. However, the means of today's wars include aerial bombardment, poison gas and even chemical weapons. And as I said there is also the potential use of the most horrific weapon of all - the nuclear bomb. Consequently, the wars of today are entirely different to those of the past, because today's wars could potentially wipe mankind from the face of the earth. Let me at this point present a beautiful teaching of the Holy Qur'an regarding the establishment of peace. The Qur'an says:

And good and evil are not alike. Repel *evil* with that which is best. And lo, he, between whom and thyself was enmity, will become as though he were a warm friend. (ch. 41: v. 35)

Thus, the Qur'an teaches that as far as possible, any enmities or grudges should be reconciled and solved by opening the channels of communication and through dialogue. Most certainly to speak to someone with kindness and wisdom can only have a very positive and endearing effect on their heart and is a means of removing hatred and grudges.

No doubt, we in this era believe ourselves to be extremely

advanced and civilised. We have created various international charities and foundations that provide healthcare and education to children or that provide healthcare to mothers. Similarly, there are countless other charities established out of human sympathy and compassion. We, who have done all of this, should reflect and pay attention to the urgent need of the time and contemplate how we can save ourselves and others from devastation and destruction. We should remember that compared to six or seven decades ago the world is now much closer together. Sixty or seventy years ago New Zealand was a distant country, far away from Asia and Europe. However, today it is an integral part of one common global community. Thus, in a state of war, no country and no region is safe.

Your leaders and your politicians are the guardians of the nation. They are responsible for the safety of the country and for its continued progress and betterment. And so it is essential that they always keep in mind the critical point that it is from local wars that devastation and destruction spreads far and wide. We should be grateful to God that He recently granted sense and wisdom to some of the major powers so that they realised that they had to take action to stop war to prevent the utter devastation that would have ensued. Most pertinently, Russia's President made efforts to hold back some of the other major powers from attacking Syria. He made it clear that all countries, whether large or small, should be treated equally. He also said that if the requirements of justice were not met and if other nations went to war independently then the United Nations would suffer the same sorry fate as the League of Nations. I believe that he was completely correct in this analysis. Although I do not support all of his policies, but a word of wisdom ought to be accepted. I wish only that he had gone one step further and said that the right of veto power held by the five permanent members of the UN Security Council should be ended once and for all so that true justice and equity could prevail amongst all nations.

Last year, I was given the opportunity to make an address at Capitol Hill in Washington D.C. The audience included numerous Senators, Congressmen, think-tank representatives and many other educated people from various fields. I clearly said to them that the requirements of justice are only fulfilled when all parties and all people are treated equally. I said to them that if you want to highlight the differences between the large and small countries and the rich and poor nations and if you want to maintain the injustice of veto power, then restlessness and anxiety will certainly develop. Indeed such anxieties have already begun to show their face in the world.

And so, as the Head of a worldwide Muslim community, it is my duty that I should draw the attention of the world towards establishing peace. I consider this my obligation because Islam's very meaning is peace and security. If certain Muslim countries carry out or promote hate-filled acts of extremism it should not lead to the conclusion that Islamic teachings promote disorder or strife. I have just quoted a verse of the Holy Qur'an and within it is a lesson of how to establish peace.

Furthermore, the Founder of Islam, the Holy Prophet Muhammad[sa] taught his followers to always give "salaam," meaning to always spread the message of peace. We know from his blessed example that he would invoke peace to all non-Muslims, be they Jews, Christians or the people of any other faiths or beliefs. He did so because he understood that all people formed part of God's Creation, and because one of God's names is the "Source of Peace" and so He desires peace and security for all of mankind.

I have mentioned some of Islam's teachings in relation to peace, but I should clarify that due to the lack of time I have mentioned only a few aspects. In truth, Islam is filled with commandments and teachings advocating peace and security for all people. And in relation to establishing justice what does the Qur'an say? In Chapter 5, Verse 9, Allah says:

> O ye who believe! Be steadfast in the cause of Allah, bearing witness in equity; and let not a people's enmity incite you to act otherwise than with justice. Be *always* just, that is nearer to righteousness. And fear Allah. Surely, Allah is Aware of what you do.

And so in this verse the Qur'an outlines the very highest possible standards of justice. This commandment leaves no room for people who call themselves Muslims yet who commit atrocities and brutalities. Neither does it leave any room for criticism from those people who consider or seek to portray Islam as a violent and extremist religion. The Qur'an has further laid down the most exemplary standards of justice and fairness. It has not only said to be just, but in fact advocates equity to such an extent that it states:

> O ye who believe! Be strict in observing justice, *and be* witnesses for Allah, even though it be *against* yourselves or against parents and *your* kindred. Whether he, against whom witness is borne, be rich or poor, Allah is more

regardful of them both *than you are*. Therefore do not follow your low desires that you may *be able* to act equitably. And if you hide *the truth* or evade *it*, then *know that* Allah is Well-Aware of what you do. (ch. 4: v. 136)

And so it is such principled standards of justice that establish peace in the world, from the most basic element of society all the way through to the international arena. History testifies to the fact that the Founder of Islam, the Holy Prophet Muhammad[sa], acted upon this teaching and spread it to all corners. And now in this era, the true devotee of the Holy Prophet[sa], who was the Founder of the Ahmadiyya Muslim Jamā'at (Community), Ḥaḍrat Mirza Ghulam Ahmad[as] of Qadian, spread and championed this teaching and instructed his followers to also spread peace. He further instructed his followers to draw the attention of mankind towards fulfilling both the rights of God and the rights of God's creation. It is for this reason that the Ahmadiyya Community emphasises to all people the critical need of fulfilling the rights of Allah and of His creation and of establishing the very best standards of justice. It is my prayer that every single one of us, irrespective of religion or belief, pays heed towards fulfilling each other's due rights, so that the world can become a haven of peace and harmony.

With these few words I conclude and I thank you once again for inviting me and coming here to listen to me.

WORLD PEACE & SECURITY—
THE CRITICAL ISSUES OF OUR TIME

DUTCH NATIONAL PARLIAMENT
BINNENHOF, THE HAGUE, NETHERLANDS, 2015

Ḥaḍrat Khalifatul-Masiḥ V[aba] at a special session of the Standing Committee for Foreign Affairs at the Netherlands National Parliament.

Members of the Standing Committee for Foreign Affairs at the Netherlands National Parliament with Ḥaḍrat Khalifatul-Masiḥ V[aba]

Ḥaḍrat Khalifatul-Masiḥ V[aba] delivering his historic address at a special session
of the Standing Committee for Foreign Affairs at the Netherlands National Parliament.

Ḥaḍrat Khalifatul-Masiḥ V[aba] answering a question about a range of political and religious issues.

Preface

On 6 October 2015, Worldwide Head of the Ahmadiyya Muslim Community, the Fifth *Khalīfah* (Caliph), His Holiness, Ḥaḍrat Mirza Masroor Ahmad[aba], delivered an historic address at a special session of the Standing Committee for Foreign Affairs at the Netherlands National Parliament in the country's capital city of Den Haag (The Hague) in front of an audience of more than 100 dignitaries and guests. The formal session commenced as Mr. Van Bommel welcomed His Holiness to Parliament and introduced the committee members. He also welcomed various foreign Parliamentarians, Ambassadors of State and dignitaries representing countries including Albania, Croatia, Ireland, Montenegro, Spain and Sweden.

World Peace & Security—
The Critical Issues of Our Time

Ḥaḍrat Mirza Masroor Ahmad, Khalīfatul-Masīḥ V^{aba} said:

Bismillāhir-Raḥmānir-Raḥīm—In the name of Allah, the Gracious, Ever Merciful.

All distinguished guests, peace and blessings of Allah be upon you. First of all, I would like to take this opportunity to sincerely express my gratitude to the organisers of today's event for inviting me to address this gathering.

In today's world we see that certain issues are constantly being highlighted and labelled as the most significant problems of our time. For example, some people are emphasising the threat of global warming and climate change.

Then, there are some who are extremely concerned about the escalation of various conflicts and the increasingly volatile state of the world. If we analyse the situation objectively, we realise that world peace and security is indeed the most critical issue of our time. Unquestionably, with each day that passes the world is becoming increasingly unstable and dangerous and there are a number of potential causes of this. For example, the financial crisis and economic instability that has affected many parts of the world may be one major factor.

Another possible root cause is the lack of justice displayed by certain world leaders towards their own people and towards others. A further reason may be the fact that some religious leaders are prioritising their own personal interests above the greater collective good and are not discharging their responsibilities with sincerity. In terms of international relations, a major source of conflict may well be the discrepancy between the rich and poor nations of the world.

It is observed that powerful nations often seek to benefit from the natural resources of poor nations without giving them the appropriate share of their own assets. Thus, there is a long list of possible reasons as to why the peace of the world is being disturbed, of which I have mentioned just a few. Whatever the causes, I certainly believe the lack of peace in the world to be the most precarious issue of this generation.

Upon hearing this, many of you may respond by saying that it is in Muslim countries where we see the most instability and the world's lack of peace is rooted in the disorder we see in Muslim world.

Indeed, because I am the leader of one of the worldwide Muslim communities—the Ahmadiyya Muslim Community—perhaps you will consider that I too bear some responsibility for this. You may also believe that the birth of extremist groups and the rise of terrorism is actually inspired by Islamic teachings. However, it is entirely unjust to associate Islam with such disorder and hatred.

At this time, there is no need to speak in detail about the history of religions, but suffice to say that if we look at the history of all religions objectively, we see that over time the followers of every religion moved away from the original teachings and this led to internal division and conflicts. People were killed and great cruelties were inflicted.

Keeping this in view, I wholeheartedly accept that over time Muslims have also moved away from Islam's true teachings. This led to frustrations and rivalries developing, which in turn have led to sectarianism, violence and injustice. However, from the perspective of a true Muslim, my faith does not decrease upon observing the desperate state of Islam today.

This is because over 1400 years ago the Founder of Islam, the Holy Prophet Muhammad (peace be upon him) prophesied that gradually Islam's teachings would become corrupted and Muslims would enter into an age of moral decline. However, he also foretold that at such a time of spiritual darkness, a Reformer would be sent by God Almighty, as the Promised Messiah and Imam Mahdi[as], to guide mankind back towards the true and peaceful teachings of Islam.

As foretold by the Holy Prophet (peace be upon him), the Promised Messiah (peace be upon him) enlightened us with the original and entirely peaceful teachings of Islam. Thus we Ahmadi Muslims, are not amongst those people who are creating or partaking in today's disorder and unrest. Rather, we are the people who desire peace in the world.

We are the people who seek to heal the world. We are the people who seek to unite mankind. We are the people who seek to transform all hatreds and enmities into love and affection. And most certainly, we are the people who make every possible effort towards establishing world peace. As a religious leader, I wish to say that instead of blaming and provoking one another, we should focus upon building true and long-lasting world peace.

In this regard the Founder of the Ahmadiyya Muslim Community, has informed us of a vital principle. He said that to establish peace it was essential that mankind sought to adopt and follow the Attributes of God Almighty to the best of their abilities. He said that this was the way to ensure the continued well-being of mankind. Indeed, he further explained that the welfare and prosperity of humanity, both physically and spiritually, was directly linked to observing the Attributes of God Almighty, because it was through His Attributes that all forms of peace emanated.

This is reflected in the very first verse of the Holy Qur'an where it states that Allah is He who is 'Lord of All the Worlds'. This means that He is the Provider, Sustainer and Master of every single person and of every form of Creation. He is not only the Lord of the Muslims, but He is the Lord of the Christians, the Jews, and the Hindus and indeed of all people - no matter their religion or beliefs.

God's love and benevolence towards His Creation is incomparable and unique. He is also the Gracious and Merciful. He is the Source of Peace. Thus, when Islam stipulates that a Muslim should seek to inculcate the Attributes of God Almighty, it becomes impossible for a true Muslim to harm others. Rather, the faith of a true Muslim compels him to love all of mankind and to treat every person with respect, grace and sympathy.

It is often queried that if Islam is a religion of peace, then why has the Qur'an given permission for war? However, that permission must be understood in its correct context and in light of what I have just explained. Maintaining long-lasting peace is of paramount importance and value. And, on certain occasions punishments or warnings are also required in order to ensure long-term peace.

Accordingly, when permission for warfare was given by Allah the Almighty, it was given as a means of restoring peace and only as a defensive measure. Thus, it is an injustice of the very highest order that certain groups or individuals seek to associate the Holy Qur'an and the Holy Prophet (peace be upon him) with violence or cruelty. If we study the Holy Qur'an and the life of the Holy Prophet (peace be upon him) in an impartial way then we see that Islam is completely against all forms of extremism and bloodshed.

Due to the limitations of time, I cannot speak in detail but nonetheless, I will mention certain basic Islamic teachings, which prove beyond doubt that Islam is a religion of peace. As I just said, a basic and common allegation levelled at Islam's door is that it is a religion that promotes extremism and warfare. However nothing could be further from the truth.

Thus, in chapter 2, verse 191, Allah has commanded that war can only ever be justified as a means of defence. This point is reiterated in chapter 22, verse 40, which categorically states that permission for war is given only to those who have been attacked and upon whom war is forced. Further, where Allah the Almighty has given Muslim governments permission for war, it has been given

only as a means to secure religious freedom and freedom of belief.
Thus, in chapter 2, verse 194, Allah has commanded Muslims that
they are not permitted to engage in any battle or war where religious freedom already exists.

Therefore, no Muslim country, group or individual has the
right to engage in any form of violence, warfare or lawlessness,
either against the state or its people. Quite simply, in Europe and
in the West, the governments are secular and so a Muslim can
never have the right to violate the laws of the land, to violently
oppose the government or to instigate any form of rebellion or
insurgency.

In fact, according to the true teachings of Islam, even if a
person considers that he or she does not have true religious freedom, whilst living in a non-Muslim country, they must not engage
in dissent or lawlessness; rather, they should leave that country
and migrate to a place with more favourable conditions.

In chapter 16, verse 127 of the Holy Qur'an, Muslim governments have been commanded that if they are ever attacked they
must respond proportionately and only to the extent of self-de-
fence. Thus, the Qur'an is very clear that punishment should be
limited and proportionate to the crime committed. In chapter 8,
verse 62 of the Holy Qur'an, Allah has said that if your opponents
have ill-intent and are planning to harm you, but thereafter decide
to desist and move towards reconciliation, you must immediately
accept their gesture and work towards a peaceful resolution, no
matter what their motivation is.

This Qur'anic teaching is a key principle for maintaining international peace and security. In today's world, there are many
examples where countries have chosen to develop very aggressive

policies in response to the perceived hostility of others. It seems they act upon the principle that 'it is better to destroy them, before they destroy us.'

However, Islam teaches that no opportunity for peace should be wasted and so even if there is only a glimmer of hope then you must try and grasp it. In chapter 5, verse 9, Allah the Almighty has proclaimed that the enmity of a nation or people should never incite you to act otherwise than with justice and fairness. Islam teaches that in all circumstances, no matter how difficult, you must remain firmly attached to the principles of justice and integrity. Thus, even in a state of war, justice and fairness are of paramount importance and when a war concludes, the victor must continue to be just and never resort to undue cruelty.

However, in today's world we do not find such high moral standards and levels of integrity; rather, after a war is finished, countries impose sanctions and restrictions that limit the progress of the defeated parties and prevent their nations from attaining true freedom or independence. Such policies are harming international relations and can only ever increase frustrations and have a negative impact.

The truth is that sustainable peace can never be established until there is justice at every level of society. Another important teaching of Islam, which we find in chapter 8, verse 68 of the Holy Qur'an, states that Muslims are not permitted to take prisoners outside of a state of war. Hence, extremist and terrorist groups who are taking prisoners for no reason, are acting completely against the teachings of Islam. Indeed, according to reports, they are not just taking prisoners, but are also inflicting the most barbaric cruelties upon their victims.

What these terrorist groups are doing can only be condemned in the strongest possible terms. On the other hand, the Qur'an teaches that even where prisoners are justifiably taken, it is better to exhibit favour upon them and to release them wherever possible. A golden principle for the establishment of peace is given in chapter 49, verse 10 of the Holy Qur'an, where it says that if there is a dispute between nations or groups, third parties should seek to mediate and to bring about a peaceful resolution to the conflict.

In the event of an agreement, if either party unjustly seeks to subjugate the other and contravenes the negotiated settlement, then the other nations should unite together and use force if necessary to stop the aggressor. However, once the aggressive party withdraws they should not be humiliated or unduly restricted; rather, they should be permitted to move forward as a free nation and a free society. This principle is of great significance in today's world and in particular for the major powers and international organisations such as the United Nations to act upon.

In terms of establishing world peace, an extremely momentous principle, ensuring universal religious freedom, is enshrined in chapter 22, verse 41 of the Holy Qur'an. The Qur'an states that if permission for war was not granted then, in addition to mosques, churches, synagogues, temples and the places of worship of all religions would be in grave danger. Thus, where Allah the Almighty permitted the use of force, it was not just to save Islam, but to save religion itself.

In truth, Islam guarantees the freedom, liberty and protection of the people of all religions. Islam protects the right of every individual to follow his or her own chosen path or belief. I have narrated before you just a few points from the Holy Qur'an, which are the means for fostering unity at all levels of society and in all parts of the world. These are the golden keys to peace that the Holy Qur'an has handed to the people of the world.

These are the teachings which were followed perfectly by the Holy Prophet of Islam (peace be upon him) and his true companions. And so, in conclusion, I would like to reiterate once again that the world stands in desperate need of peace and security. This is the urgent issue of our time.

All nations and all peoples must come together for the greater good and unite in their efforts to stop all forms of cruelty, persecution and injustice perpetrated in the name of religion or in any other way. This includes the mockery of any religion which can incite frustrations and resentment, and of course, also includes the hateful activities of extremist groups who are falsely justifying their evil acts in the name of religion.

Furthermore, we must be sincere with all nations and seek to help them, so that each and every country can prosper and realise its potential. The jealousies and rivalries that we are seeing are a result of a mad hunger for wealth. In this regard the Holy Qur'an has given a golden principle stating that one should not covet the wealth of others with greed. By following this teaching we can promote world peace.

At every level of society, the requirements of justice must be fulfilled, so that each person, regardless of creed, caste or colour, is able to stand upon his or her own two feet with dignity and honour. Today, we are seeing many first-world countries increasing their investments in the poorer and developing nations.

It is imperative that they act with justice and seek to help and not merely utilise their natural resources and cheap labour forces for their own national gains and profit-making. They should seek to re-invest the majority of what they earn in those countries and use the wealth to help the local people develop and to flourish.

If the developed countries act in this way, it will not just be of benefit to the poorer nations but will prove mutually beneficial. It will increase trust and confidence and remove frustrations that are building up.

It will eradicate the impression that the wealthy nations care only for themselves and desire to unjustly derive benefit from the resources of the weak and poor. Furthermore, it will be a means of improving the local economies and so in turn will elevate the world's economy and financial health.

Most certainly, it would be a means of establishing a sense of global community, compassion and humanity. And above all it will be the foundations for true peace in the world. If we do not pay heed to this then the state of today's world peace will lead to the outbreak of a disastrous world war whose repercussion will be felt for generations to come and consequently our generations won't forgive us for this.

With these words, I would now like to take your leave. May Allah enable for true peace to emerge in the world.

Thank you very much.

THE KEYS TO PEACE
IN A TIME OF GLOBAL DISORDER

TOKYO, JAPAN, 2015

Ḥaḍrat Khalifatul-Masiḥ V[aba] leading silent prayer at a special reception in Tokyo, Japan.

Ḥaḍrat Khalifatul-Masiḥ V[aba] watering a plant at a special reception in Tokyo, Japan.

Ḥaḍrat Khalifatul-Masiḥ V[aba] delivering keynote address at a special reception in Tokyo, Japan.

Preface

On 23 November 2015, the Worldwide Head of the Ahmadiyya Muslim Community, the Fifth *Khalīfah* (Caliph), His Holiness, Ḥaḍrat Mirza Masroor Ahmad[aba], delivered the keynote address at a special reception held in his honour at the Hilton Hotel in Odaiba, Tokyo. More than 60 guests attended the reception, during which His Holiness reflected upon the nuclear attacks that took place in Hiroshima and Nagasaki 70 years ago. Earlier in the evening two guest speakers also addressed the audience, Dr. Mike Sata Yasuhiko PhD, Chairman Tokibo group of industries and Mr. Endo Shinichi, from Tohoku, the region most affected by the 2011 earthquake and tsunamis.

The Keys to Peace in a Time of Global Disorder

After reciting *tashahhud, taʻawwudh and bismillāh,* Ḥaḍrat Khalīfatul-Masīḥ V[aba] said:

All distinguished guests—*assalāmo ʻalaikum wa raḥmatullāhe wa barakātohū*—peace and blessings of Allah be upon you all.

First of all I would like to take this opportunity to thank all of our guests who have accepted our invitation to today's event. We are living in extremely precarious and dangerous times, in which the state of the world is a cause of huge concern. Conflict and disorder is consuming the world and threatening international peace and security.

If we glance towards the Muslim world we see that in a number of countries the governments are involved in brutal wars with their own people. Bloodshed and senseless violence is completely destroying the fabric of those nations. Terrorist groups are taking advantage of the resulting power vacuums by taking control of certain areas and establishing their own so-called governments and rule. They are acting in a heinous fashion and committing the most barbaric cruelties imaginable, not only in their own countries, but they have now also reached Europe and the recent example of their brutalities is the Paris attacks.

In Eastern Europe hostilities between Russia and Ukraine and other European countries are continuing to flare. Furthermore, recently there has been heightened tension between the United States and China regarding the incursion of an American warship into the South China Sea. As you are well aware there is also a long running territorial conflict between China and Japan over disputed islands.

The Kashmir issue between India and Pakistan is a constant source of conflict and shows no signs of abating. Similarly, tensions between Israel and Palestine have also destroyed the peace of the region.

In Africa, terrorist groups have gained power and control over certain regions and are causing widespread destruction and devastation. I have mentioned only a few of the issues that the world currently faces and indeed there are many further examples of discord and unrest.

Therefore, the only conclusion that can be reached is that the world is now becoming engulfed by violence and disorder. In the modern world the scope of warfare is much more vast than in previous eras. Conflicts in one part of the world do not remain limited or local, rather their effects and consequences spread much further afield.

The mass media and the means of instant communication

have transformed the world into a global village. In the olden days, it was possible for a war to remain confined to those who were directly involved, but now the consequences of each conflict and each war are truly global. In fact, for many years I have been warning that the world should realise that the effects of a war in one region can and will affect the peace and harmony of other parts of the world.

If we look back in history to the two World Wars that took place in the 20th Century, we all know that the weaponry available at that time was nowhere near as advanced or lethal as the weapons and arsenals of today. Yet still it is said that around 70 million people were killed in World War Two alone and the majority of those who lost their lives were innocent civilians. Therefore, the potential for disaster and catastrophe today is unimaginable.

At the time of the Second World War, the United States possessed nuclear weapons that, although extremely destructive, were nowhere near as powerful as modern day nuclear weapons. Furthermore, now it is not just the major powers that have nuclear bombs, but even a number of smaller countries possess them.

Whilst perhaps the major powers keep such weapons as a deterrent, there is no guarantee that the smaller countries will show such restraint. We cannot take it for granted that they will never use nuclear weapons. Thus, it is clear that the world stands on the brink of disaster.

At the end of the Second World War, your nation had to contend with the most horrific devastation and grief imaginable when hundreds of thousands of your citizens were mercilessly killed and two of your cities were demolished and destroyed in a nuclear attack that shamed humanity.

Having witnessed and borne this utterly overwhelming tragedy, the Japanese people will never desire for such an attack to ever happen again, either here in Japan, or indeed in any other part of the world. You are the people who truly understand the horrific and destructive consequences of nuclear warfare.

You are the people who know that the repercussions and after-effects of such weapons are not limited to one generation but continue for generations to come. You are the people who can testify to the unprecedented evil of nuclear weapons. Therefore, perhaps no country knows better the value of peace and security than the Japanese people.

Thankfully, Japan has recovered and is now an extremely developed nation and so keeping in view your past history, Japan must now play its role in establishing peace in the world.

Regrettably, following the conclusion of the Second World War, certain restrictions and sanctions were placed upon Japan and so it may be difficult for your nation to take huge steps or to shape the direction of the world at large.

However, your country still plays an important role in world matters and political affairs and so you should use your considerable influence in the best possible way and endeavour to bring about peace between nations and peoples.

This year marks 70 years since those desperate days in history when nuclear bombs were dropped on Hiroshima and Nagasaki inflicting utter destruction, misery and torment upon your nation.

Due to the fact you have built museums that paint an accurate picture of the devastation and carnage and due to the fact that some effects of the nuclear bombs still continue to this day, the Japanese people still understand how dangerous warfare and conflict can be.

As I alluded to earlier, the tragedy you bore was compounded by the fact that cruel and entirely unnecessary restrictions were placed upon post-war Japan. As the decades passed they will also have proved a constant reminder of the catastrophic consequences of war.

When the nuclear weapons were used against Japan, the Head of the Ahmadiyya Muslim Community at that time, who was our Second *khalīfah*, condemned the attack in the very strongest terms. He said:

Our religious and moral teachings demand of us that we proclaim before the entire world that we do not consider this horrific act and this bloodshed to be justified in any circumstances whatsoever. It makes no difference to me whether certain governments do not like what I am saying.

The Second *khalīfah* added that in the future, he did not foresee that warfare would subside; rather, he saw an escalation in violence and conflicts looming ahead.

Today, his words of warning have been proven entirely true. Although a Third World War has not been officially declared, in reality a global war is already taking place. Throughout the world men, women and children are being killed, tortured and subjected to the most heartbreaking cruelties.

As far as we are concerned, the Ahmadiyya Muslim Community has always spoken out to denounce every type of cruelty and oppression, no matter where in the world it takes place, because Islam's teachings demand that we speak out against injustice and help those who are in need or who are being maltreated. I have already mentioned how the Head of the Ahmadiyya Muslim Community at the time of the Second World War spoke out to condemn the use of the nuclear bombs against Japan.

Furthermore, a very prominent and well-known Ahmadi Muslim, who had great standing and influence in the world, took it upon himself to defend Japan and its people. I speak of Sir Chaudhry Muhammad Zafrullah Khan, who in addition to numerous other significant international posts, was Pakistan's first Foreign Minister and later became President of the United Nations General Assembly. Following the conclusion of World War Two, he spoke out and condemned attempts by certain powers to place unfair sanctions on Japan.

When addressing the 1951 San Francisco Peace Summit, as the Head of the Pakistan delegation, Chaudhry Zafrullah Khan said:

> The peace with Japan should be premised on justice and reconciliation, not on vengeance and oppression. In future Japan would play an important role as a result of the series of reforms initiated in the political and social structure of Japan, which hold out a bright promise of progress and which qualify Japan to take its place as an equal in the fellowship of peace loving nations.

His address was based on the teachings of the Holy Qur'an and the life of the Holy Prophet of Islam[sa]. Based on Islam's true teachings, he said that the victor of any war must never resort to injustice and never place unnecessary restrictions upon the vanquished party that limit their future progress and prosperity.

Chaudhry Zafrullah Khan gave this historic statement in defence of Japan because as an Ahmadi Muslim, he was not merely representing the Pakistani State, but first and foremost he was representing the exalted teachings of Islam.

And so as I have already said, you are the people who understand the consequences of warfare and cruelty more than others. Thus, at every level and in every possible way, the Japanese Government should seek to counter and prevent all forms of inhumanity, persecution and injustice. They should seek to ensure that the heinous attack they faced is never repeated again in the future anywhere in the world.

Wherever the flames of war are igniting, Japan's leaders and people should play their role in easing tensions and establishing peace. As far as Islam is concerned, there are some people who view it as a barbaric and violent religion. They support their contentions by highlighting the fact that terrorism and warfare is rampant in the Muslim world.

However, their beliefs are entirely wrong. In reality, Islam's teachings of peace are unparalleled in the history of the world. That is why our Second *khalīfah* and Chaudhry Zafrullah Khan vehemently spoke out against the atrocities committed against your nation. Very briefly, I shall now seek to explain what Islam's teachings really are.

As a fundamental principle, Islam says that any war for the sake of geo-political or economic gains or as a means to take control of natural resources can never be justified. Further, in chapter 16, verse 127 of the Holy Qur'an, Allah the Almighty has said that any punishment during a state of war must remain proportionate to the crime committed and must never exceed due limits. Following the conclusion of a war, the Qur'an says that it is better to forgive and to display patience.

Similarly, in chapter 8, verse 62, the Holy Qur'an states that where relations between two parties have broken down and preparations are made for war, if the opponents seek reconciliation, it is incumbent upon the other party to accept their gesture and to place their trust in Allah. The Qur'an says that one should not speculate about the motivation or sincerity of the opposing party, but should always work towards a peaceful resolution. This Qur'anic teaching is a key principle for maintaining international peace and security.

In chapter 5, verse 9, Allah the Almighty has proclaimed that the enmity of a nation or people should never incite you to sacrifice the principles of justice and fairness.

Rather, Islam teaches that in all circumstances, no matter how challenging, you must remain firmly attached to the principles of justice and integrity. Indeed, it is justice that is the means of improving relations, of removing frustrations and eliminating the causes of war. In chapter 24, verse 34, the Qur'an states that if after a successful war you stipulate certain fiscal dues on the captives of war as a means to set them free, your terms must be reasonable so that they can easily afford them, and if you permit them to pay in installments, it is for the better.

A golden principle for the establishment of peace is given in chapter 49, verse 10 of the Holy Qur'an, where it says that if there is a dispute between nations or groups, third parties should seek to mediate and to bring about a peaceful resolution.

In the event of an agreement, if either party unjustly contravenes the negotiated settlement, then the other nations should unite together and use force if necessary to stop the aggressor. However, once the aggressive party withdraws they should not be unduly restricted; rather, they should be permitted to move forward as an independent nation and as a free society.

This principle is of great significance in today's world and in particular for the major powers and international organisations such as the United Nations. If they act upon these values then true peace and justice can be established in the world and unnecessary frustrations will naturally die away.

Similarly, there are many other Qur'anic commandments explaining how to create peace in the world and how to end all wars. Our Gracious and Merciful Lord has given us the keys to peace because He desires for His Creation to live together harmoniously and to be free from all hatred and discord.

And so with these words, I would request all of you, to use your influence to spread peace and harmony in the world. Wherever in the world there is disorder or conflict, it is our collective obligation to stand up for justice and to strive for peace, so that we are saved from a repeat of that horrific war that took place 70 years ago and whose catastrophic consequences continued for decades and perhaps still continue today.

Whilst, on a small scale another world war has already begun, we must fulfil our duties and strive for peace before the situation escalates further and engulfs the entire world, and before those most abhorrent and deadly weapons that will destroy our future generations are utilised again.

Thus, let us fulfil our obligations and join together. Rather than grouping together in opposing blocs, we should all unite and co-operate with one another. We have no other viable option left because if a fully-fledged Third World War occurs then the resulting devastation and trail of destruction is unimaginable.

No doubt we will then consider the wars of the past to have been quite minor in comparison.

I pray that the world comes to realise the gravity of the situation before it is too late and that mankind bows down before God Almighty and fulfils His rights and the rights of one another.

May Allah grant wisdom and intelligence to those who are causing conflict in the name of religion or who are conducting wars for the sake of geo-political or economic benefits. May they come to realise how senseless and destructive their pursuits are.

And may Allah enable for true and long lasting peace to develop in all parts of the world—Ameen.

With these words I would like to once again thank you for attending today's event.

Thank you very much.

LETTERS
TO
THE WORLD LEADERS

LETTER TO HIS HOLINESS POPE BENEDICT THE XVI

بِسْمِ اللهِ الرَّحْمٰنِ الرَّحِيمِ

نَحْمَدُهُ وَ نُصَلِّى عَلَى رَسُوْلِهِ الْكَرِيْمِ

وعلى عبدهِ المسيح الموعود

خدا کے فضل اور رحم کے ساتھ

هوالناصــــر

MIRZA MASROOR AHMAD
HEAD OF THE AHMADIYYA COMMUNITY
IN ISLAM

16 Gressenhall Road
Southfields, London
SW18 5QL, UK

31 October 2011

To His Holiness Pope Benedict the XVI,

It is my prayer, that may Allah the Almighty bestow His Grace and Blessings upon you.

As Head of the worldwide Ahmadiyya Muslim Community, I convey to His Holiness the Pope the message of the Holy Qur'an: Say, '*O people of the book! Come to a word equal between us and you – that we worship none but Allah, and that we associate no partner with Him, and that some of us take not others for lords beside Allah.*'

Islam, nowadays, is under the glare of the world, and is frequently targeted with vile allegations. However, those raising these allegations do so without studying any of Islam's real teachings. Unfortunately, certain Muslim organisations due only to their vested interests have portrayed Islam in a totally wrong light. As a result, distrust has increased in the hearts of the people of Western and non-Muslim countries towards Muslims, to the extent that even otherwise extremely well-educated people make baseless allegations against the Founder of Islam, the Holy Prophet Muhammad[(pbuh)].

The purpose of every religion has been to bring man closer to God and establish human values. Never has the founder of any religion taught that his followers should usurp the rights of others or should act cruelly. Thus, the actions of a minority of misguided Muslims should not be used as a pretext to attack Islam and its Holy Founder[(pbuh)]. Islam teaches us to respect the Prophets of all religions and this is why it is essential for a Muslim to believe in all of the Prophets who are mentioned in the Holy Bible or in the Holy Qur'an, until and including Jesus Christ[(pbuh)]. We are the humble servants of the Holy Prophet Muhammad[(pbuh)] and so we are deeply grieved and saddened by the attacks on our Holy Prophet[(pbuh)]; but we respond by continuing to present his noble qualities to the world and to disclose even more of the beautiful teachings of the Holy Qur'an.

If a person does not follow a particular teaching properly whilst claiming to subscribe to it, then it is he who is in error, not the teaching. The meaning of the word 'Islam' itself means peace, love and security. *There should be no compulsion in matters of faith* is a clear injunction of the Qur'an. From cover to cover, the Holy Qur'an teaches love, affection, peace, reconciliation and the spirit of sacrifice. The Holy Qur'an states repeatedly that one who does not adopt righteousness is far removed from Allah, and therefore, is far removed from the teachings of

Islam. Hence, if anybody portrays Islam as an extreme and violent religion filled with teachings of bloodshed, then such a portrayal has no link with the real Islam.

The Ahmadiyya Muslim Community practises only the true Islam and works purely to please God Almighty. If any Church or other place of worship stands in need of protection, they will find us standing shoulder to shoulder with them. If any message resonates from our mosques it will only be that of Allah is Great and that we bear witness that there is none worthy of worship except Him and Muhammad[pbuh] is the Messenger of Allah.

A factor playing a major role in destroying the peace of the world is that some people perceive that as they are intelligent, well-educated and liberated, they are free to ridicule and mock founders of religions. To maintain peace in society it is necessary for one to eliminate all sentiments of hostility from one's heart and to increase one's levels of tolerance. There is a need to stand in defence of the respect and reverence of each other's Prophet. The world is passing through restlessness and unease and this requires that by creating an atmosphere of love and affection, we remove this anxiety and fear, that we convey a message of love and peace to those around; that we learn to live with ever greater harmony and in a way better than before; and that we recognise the values of humanity.

Today, small-scale wars are erupting in the world, while in other places, the superpowers are claiming to try and bring about peace. It is no longer a secret that on the surface we are told one thing, but behind the scenes their real priorities and policies are secretly being fulfilled. Can peace in the world be established in such circumstances is the question. It is with regret that if we now observe the current circumstances of the world closely, we find that the foundation for another world war has already been laid. If after the Second World War a path of equity leading to justice was followed, we would not witness the current state of the world, whereby it has again become engulfed in the flames of war. As a consequence of so many countries having nuclear weapons, grudges and enmities are increasing and the world sits on the precipice of destruction. If these weapons of mass destruction explode, many future generations will never forgive us for having inflicted permanent disabilities upon them. There is still time for the world to pay attention to the rights of the Creator and of His Creatures.

I believe that now, rather than focusing on the *progress* of the world, it is more important, indeed it is essential, that we urgently increase our efforts to *save* the world from this destruction. There is an urgent need for mankind to recognise its Creator as this is the only guarantor for the survival of humanity; otherwise, the world is rapidly moving towards self-destruction. If today man really wants to be successful in establishing peace, then instead of finding fault with others, he should try to control the Satan within. By removing his own evils, a person should present a wonderful example of justice. I frequently remind the world that these excessive enmities towards others are completely usurping human values and so are leading the world towards obliteration.

As you have an influential voice in the world, I urge you to also inform the wider world that by placing obstacles in the way of the natural balance established by God, they are moving rapidly towards annihilation. This message needs to be conveyed further and wider than ever before and with much greater prominence.

All the religions of the world are in need of religious harmony and all the people of the world need a spirit of love, affection and brotherhood to be created. It is my prayer that we all understand our responsibilities and play our role in establishing peace and love, and for the recognition of our Creator in the world. We ourselves have prayer, and we constantly beseech Allah that may this destruction of the world be avoided. I pray that we are saved from the destruction that awaits us.

Yours sincerely,

Mirza Masroor Ahmad
Khalifatul Masih V
Head of the Worldwide
Ahmadiyya Muslim Community

LETTER TO THE PRIME MINISTER
OF ISRAEL

بِسْمِ اللهِ الرَّحْمٰنِ الرَّحِيْمِ

نَحْمَدُهُ وَ نُصَلِّى عَلٰى رَسُوْلِهِ الْكَرِيْمِ

وعلى عبدِهِ المسيح الموعود

خدا کے فضل اور رحم کے ساتھ

هو الناصـــر

MIRZA MASROOR AHMAD
HEAD OF THE AHMADIYYA COMMUNITY
IN ISLAM

16 Gressenhall Road
Southfields, London
SW18 5QL, UK

His Excellency
Mr Benjamin Netanyahu
Prime Minister of Israel
Jerusalem

26 February 2012

Dear Prime Minister,

I recently sent a letter to His Excellency Shimon Peres, President of Israel, regarding the perilous state of affairs emerging in the world. In light of the rapidly changing circumstances, I felt it was essential for me to convey my message to you also, as you are the Head of the Government of your country.

The history of your nation is closely linked with prophethood and Divine revelation. Indeed, the Prophets of the Children of Israel made very clear prophecies regarding your nation's future. As a result of disobedience to the teachings of the Prophets and negligence towards their prophecies, the Children of Israel had to suffer difficulties and tribulations. If the leaders of your nation had remained firm in obedience to the Prophets, they could have been saved from enduring various misfortunes and adversities. Thus, it is your duty, perhaps even more so than others, to pay heed to the prophecies and injunctions of the Prophets.

I address you as the Khalifa of that Promised Messiah and Imam Mahdi (peace be upon him), who was sent as the servant of the Holy Prophet Muhammad (peace and blessings of Allah be upon him); and the Holy Prophet (peace and blessings of Allah be upon him) was sent as the Mercy for All Mankind amongst the brethren of the Children of Israel in the semblance of Moses (peace be upon him) (Deuteronomy, 18:18). Hence, it is my duty to remind you of God's Message. I hope that you will come to be counted amongst those who hearken to God's Call, and who successfully find the right path; that path which is in accordance with the Guidance of God the Supreme, the Master of the heavens and the earth.

We hear reports in the news nowadays that you are preparing to attack Iran. Yet the horrific outcome of a World War is right before you. In the last World War, whilst millions of other people were killed, the lives of hundreds of thousands of Jewish persons were also wasted. As the Prime Minister, it is your duty to protect the life of your nation. The current circumstances of the world indicate that a World War will not be fought between only two countries, rather blocs will come into formation. The threat of a World War breaking out is a very serious one. The life of Muslims, Christians and Jews are all at peril from it. If such a war occurs, it will result in a chain reaction of human destruction. The effects of this catastrophe will be felt by future generations, who will either be born disabled, or crippled. This is because undoubtedly, such a war will involve atomic warfare.

Hence, it is my request to you that instead of leading the world into the grip of a World War, make maximum efforts to save the world from a global catastrophe. Instead of resolving disputes with force, you should try to resolve them through dialogue, so that we can gift our future generations with a bright future rather than 'gift' them with disability and defects.

I shall try to elucidate my views based on the following passages from your teachings, the first extract being from the Zabur:

'Do not fret because of evil-doers. Do not envy those who do wrong. For they shall soon be cut down like the grass, and wither like the green herb. Trust in God, and do good. Dwell in the land, and enjoy safe pasture. Also delight yourself in God, and he will give you the desires of your heart. Commit your way to God. Trust also in him, and he will do this: He will make your righteousness go forth as the dawn, and your justice as the noon day sun. Rest in God, and wait patiently for him. Do not fret because of him who prospers in his way, because of the man who makes wicked plots happen. Cease from anger, and forsake wrath. Do not fret, it leads only to evildoing. For evildoers shall be cut off, but those who wait for God shall inherit the land. For yet a little while, and the wicked will be no more. Yes, though you look for his place, he is not there. But the humble shall inherit the land, and shall delight themselves in the abundance of peace.' (Zabur, 37:1-11)

Similarly, we find in the Torah:

'Thou shalt not have in thy bag divers weights, a great and a small. Thou shalt not have in thine house divers measures, a great and a small. [But] thou shalt have a perfect and just weight, a perfect and just measure shalt thou have: that thy days may be lengthened in the land which the LORD thy God giveth thee. For all that do such things, [and] all that do unrighteously, [are] an abomination unto the LORD thy God.' (Deuteronomy, 25:13-16)

Thus, world leaders, and particularly you should terminate the notion of governance by force and should refrain from oppressing the weak. Instead, strive to spread and promote justice and peace. By doing so, you will remain in peace yourselves, you will gain strength and world peace will also be established.

It is my prayer that you and other world leaders understand my message, recognise your station and status and fulfil your responsibilities.

Yours Sincerely,

MIRZA MASROOR AHMAD
Khalifatul Masih V
Head of the Worldwide Ahmadiyya Muslim Community

LETTER TO THE PRESIDENT OF
THE ISLAMIC REPUBLIC OF IRAN

بِسْمِ اللهِ الرَّحْمٰنِ الرَّحِيْمِ

نَحْمَدُهُ وَ نُصَلِّی عَلٰی رَسُوْلِهِ الْکَرِیْمِ

وَعَلٰی عَبْدِهِ الْمَسِیْحِ الْمَوْعُوْدِ

خدا کے فضل اور رحم کے ساتھ

هو النَّاصِرِ

MIRZA MASROOR AHMAD
HEAD OF THE AHMADIYYA COMMUNITY
IN ISLAM

16 Gressenhall Road
Southfields, London
SW18 5QL, UK

His Excellency
President of the Islamic Republic of Iran
Mahmoud Ahmadinejad
Tehran

7 March 2012

Dear Mr President,

Assalamo Alaikum Wa Rahmatullahe Wa Barakatohu,

In light of the perilous state of affairs emerging in the world, I felt that it was essential for me to write to you, as you are the President of Iran, and thus you hold the authority to make decisions which will affect the future of your nation and the world at large. There is currently great agitation and restlessness in the world. In some areas small-scale wars have broken out, while in other places the superpowers act on the pretext of trying to bring about peace. Each country is engaged in activities to either help or oppose other countries, but the requirements of justice are not being fulfilled. It is with regret that if we now observe the current circumstances of the world, we find that the foundation for another world war has already been laid. As so many countries, both large and small, have nuclear weapons, grudges and hostilities are increasing. In such a predicament, the Third World War looms almost certainly before us. As you are aware, the availability of nuclear weapons will mean that a Third World War will be an atomic war. Its ultimate result will be catastrophic, and the long term effects of such warfare could lead to future generations being born disabled or deformed.

It is my belief that as followers of the Holy Prophet Muhammad[(pbuh)], who was sent to establish peace in the world, and who was the *Rahmatullil Aalameen* – the Mercy to all of Mankind –we do not and cannot desire for the world to suffer such a fate. This is why my request to you is that as Iran is also a significant power in the world, it should play its role to prevent a Third World War. It is undeniably true that the major powers act with double standards. Their injustices have caused restlessness and disorder to spread all across the world. However, we cannot ignore the fact that some Muslim groups act inappropriately, and contrary to the teachings of Islam. Major world powers have used this as a pretext to fulfil their vested interests by taking advantage of the poor Muslim countries. Thus, I request you once again, that you should focus all of your efforts and energies towards saving the world from a Third World War. The Holy Qur'an teaches Muslims that enmity against any nation should not hinder them from acting in a just manner. In *Surah Al Mai'dah*, Allah the Exalted instructs us:

"And let not the enmity of a people, that they hindered you from the Sacred Mosque, incite you to transgress. And help one another in righteousness and piety; but help not one another in sin and transgression. And fear Allah; surely, Allah is severe in punishment." (Ch.5:V.3)

Similarly, in the same chapter of the Holy Qur'an we find the following commandment to Muslims:

"O ye who believe! Be steadfast in the cause of Allah, bearing witness in equity; and let not a people's enmity incite you to act otherwise than with justice. Be always just, that is nearer to righteousness. And fear Allah. Surely, Allah is aware of what you do."(Ch.5:V.9)

Hence, you should not oppose another nation merely out of enmity and hatred. I admit that Israel exceeds beyond its limits, and has its eyes cast upon Iran. Indeed, if any country transgresses against your country, naturally you have the right to defend yourself. However, as far as possible disputes should be resolved through diplomacy and negotiations. This is my humble request to you, that rather than using force, use dialogue to try and resolve conflicts. The reason why I make this request is because I am the follower of that Chosen Person of God who came in this era as the True Servant of the Holy Prophet Muhammad[pbuh], and who claimed to be the Promised Messiah and Imam Mahdi. His mission was to bring mankind closer to God and to establish the rights of people in the manner our Master and Guide, the *Rahmatullil Aalameen* –the Mercy to all of Mankind – the Holy Prophet[pbuh] demonstrated to us. May Allah the Exalted enable the Muslim *Ummah* to understand this beautiful teaching.

Wassalam,

Yours Sincerely,

MIRZA MASROOR AHMAD
Khalifatul Masih V
Head of the Worldwide Ahmadiyya Muslim Community

LETTER TO THE PRESIDENT OF THE UNITED STATES OF AMERICA

بِسْمِ اللهِ الرَّحْمٰنِ الرَّحِيْمِ

نَحْمَدُهُ وَ نُصَلِّى عَلٰى رَسُوْلِهِ الْكَرِيْمِ

وعلٰى عبدِهِ المسيح الموعود

خدا کے فضل اور رحم کے ساتھ

هو الناصر

MIRZA MASROOR AHMAD
HEAD OF THE AHMADIYYA COMMUNITY
IN ISLAM

16 Gressenhall Road
Southfields, London
SW18 5QL, UK

President Barack Obama
President of the United States of America
The White House
1600 Pennsylvania Avenue NW
Washington D.C.

8 March 2012

Dear Mr President,

In light of the perturbing state of affairs developing in the world, I felt that it was necessary for me to write to you, as you are the President of the United States of America, a country which is a world superpower, and thus you hold the authority to make decisions which will affect the future of your nation and the world at large.

There is currently great agitation and restlessness in the world. Small-scale wars have broken out in certain areas. Unfortunately, the superpowers have not been as successful as was anticipated in their efforts to establish peace in these conflict-hit regions. Globally, we find that almost every country is engaged in activities to either support, or oppose other countries; however, the requirements of justice are not being fulfilled. It is with regret that if we now observe the current circumstances of the world, we find that the foundation for another world war has already been laid. As so many countries, both large and small, have nuclear weapons, grudges and hostilities are increasing between nations. In such a predicament, the Third World War looms almost certainly before us. Such a war would surely involve atomic warfare; and therefore, we are witnessing the world head towards a terrifying destruction. If a path of equity and justice had been followed after the Second World War, we would not be witnessing the current state of the world today whereby it has become engulfed in the flames of war once again.

As we are all aware, the main causes that led to the Second World War were the failure of League of Nations and the economic crisis, which began in 1932. Today, leading economists state that there are numerous parallels between the current economic crisis and that of 1932. We observe that political and economic problems have once again led to wars between smaller nations, and to internal discord and discontentment becoming rife within these countries. This will ultimately result in certain powers emerging to the helm of government, who will lead us to a world war. If in the smaller countries conflicts cannot be resolved through politics or diplomacy, it will lead to new blocs and groupings to form in the world. This will be the precursor for the outbreak of a Third World War. Hence, I believe that now, rather than focusing on the *progress* of the world, it is more important and indeed essential, that we urgently increase our efforts to *save* the world from this destruction. There is an urgent need for mankind to recognise its One God, Who is our Creator, as this is the only guarantor for the survival of humanity; otherwise, the world will continue to rapidly head towards self-destruction.

My request to you, and indeed to all world leaders, is that instead of using force to suppress other nations, use diplomacy, dialogue and wisdom. The major powers of the world, such as the United States, should play their role towards establishing peace. They should not use the acts of smaller countries as a pretext to disturb world harmony. Currently, nuclear arms are not only possessed by the United States and other major powers; rather, even relatively smaller countries now possess such weapons of mass destruction, where those who are in power are often trigger-happy leaders who act without thought or consideration. Thus, it is my humble request to you to strive to your utmost to prevent the major and minor powers from erupting into a Third World War. There should be no doubt in our minds that if we fail in this task then the effects and aftermath of such a war will not be limited to only the poor countries of Asia, Europe and the Americas; rather, our future generations will have to bear the horrific consequences of our actions and children everywhere in the world will be born disabled or deformed. They will never forgive their elders who led the world to a global catastrophe. Instead of being concerned for only our vested interests, we should consider our coming generations and strive to create a brighter future for them. May God the Exalted enable you, and all world leaders, to comprehend this message.

Yours Sincerely,

MIRZA MASROOR AHMAD
Khalifatul Masih V
Head of the Worldwide Ahmadiyya Muslim Community

LETTER TO THE
PRIME MINISTER OF CANADA

بِسْمِ اللهِ الرَّحْمٰنِ الرَّحِيْمِ

نَحْمَدُهُ وَ نُصَلِّى عَلٰى رَسُوْلِهِ الْكَرِيْمِ

وعلٰى عبدِهِ المَسيح المَوعود

خدا کے فضل اور رحم کے ساتھ

هوالناصـــــر

MIRZA MASROOR AHMAD
HEAD OF THE AHMADIYYA COMMUNITY
IN ISLAM

16 Gressenhall Road
Southfields, London
SW18 5QL, UK

Mr. Stephen Harper
Prime Minster of Canada
Ottawa, Ontario

8 March 2012

Dear Prime Minister,

In light of the dire state of affairs developing in the world, I felt that it was necessary for me to write to you, as you are the Prime Minister of Canada, and hence you hold the authority to make decisions which will affect the future of your nation and the world at large. There is currently great agitation and restlessness in the world. Small-scale wars have broken out in certain areas. Unfortunately, the superpowers have not been as successful as was anticipated in their efforts to establish peace in these conflict-hit regions. Globally, we find that almost every country is engaged in activities to either support, or oppose other countries; however, the requirements of justice are not being fulfilled. It is with regret that if we now observe the current circumstances of the world, we find that the foundation for another world war has already been laid. As so many countries, both large and small, have nuclear weapons, grudges and hostilities are increasing between nations. In such a predicament, the Third World War looms almost certainly before us. Such a war would surely involve atomic warfare; and therefore, we are witnessing the world head towards a terrifying destruction. If a path of equity and justice had been followed after the Second World War, we would not be witnessing the current state of the world today whereby it has become engulfed in the flames of war once again.

As we are all aware, the main causes that led to the Second World War were the failure of League of Nations and the economic crisis, which began in 1932. Today, leading economists state that there are numerous parallels between the current economic crisis and that of 1932. We observe that political and economic problems have once again led to wars between smaller nations, and to internal discord and discontentment becoming rife within these countries. This will ultimately result in certain powers emerging to the helm of government, who will lead us to a world war. If in the smaller countries conflicts cannot be resolved through politics or diplomacy, it will lead to new blocs and grouping to form in the world. This will be the precursor for the outbreak of a Third World War. Hence, I believe that now, rather than focusing on the *progress* of the world, it is more important and indeed essential, that we urgently increase our efforts to *save* the world from this destruction. There is an urgent need for mankind to recognise its One God, Who is our Creator, as this is the only guarantor for the survival of humanity; otherwise, the world will continue to rapidly head towards self-destruction.

Canada is widely considered to be one of the most just countries in the world. Your nation does not normally interfere in the internal problems of other countries. Further, we, the Ahmadiyya Muslim Community, have special ties of friendship with the people of Canada. Thus, I request you to strive to your utmost to prevent the major and minor powers from leading us into a devastating Third World War.

My request to you, and indeed to all world leaders, is that instead of using force to suppress other nations, use diplomacy, dialogue and wisdom. The major powers of the world, such as Canada, should play their role towards establishing peace. They should not use the acts of smaller countries as a pretext to disturb world harmony. Currently, nuclear arms are not only possessed by the major world powers, rather even relatively smaller countries now possess such weapons of mass destruction; where those who are in power are often trigger-happy leaders who act without thought or consideration. Thus, it is my humble request to you that use all your energy and efforts to prevent a Third World War from occurring. There should be no doubts in our minds that if we fail in this task then the effects and aftermath of such a war, will not be limited to only the poor countries of Asia, Europe and the Americas; rather, our future generations will have to bear the horrific consequences of our actions and children everywhere in the world will be born disabled or deformed. They will never forgive their elders who led the world to a global catastrophe. Instead of being concerned for only our vested interests, we should consider our coming generations and strive to create a brighter future for them. May God the Exalted enable you, and all world leaders, to comprehend this message.

Yours Sincerely,

MIRZA MASROOR AHMAD
Khalifatul Masih V
Head of the Worldwide Ahmadiyya Muslim Community

LETTER TO THE CUSTODIAN OF THE TWO HOLY PLACES THE KING OF THE KINGDOM OF SAUDI ARABIA

MIRZA MASROOR AHMAD
HEAD OF THE AHMADIYYA COMMUNITY
IN ISLAM

بِسْمِ اللهِ الرَّحْمٰنِ الرَّحِيْمِ

نَحْمَدُهُ وَ نُصَلِّي عَلَى رَسُوْلِهِ الْكَرِيْمِ

وعلى عبده المسيح الموعود

خدا کے فضل اور رحم کے ساتھ

هو الناصر

16 Gressenhall Road
Southfields, London
SW18 5QL, UK

Custodian of the Two Holy Places
King of the Kingdom of Saudi Arabia
Abdullah bin Abdul-Aziz Al Saud
Riyadh, Saudi Arabia

28 March 2012

Respected King Abdullah,

Assalamo Alaikum Wa Rahmatullahe Wa Barakatohu,

Today, I am writing to you with the intention of raising a most important matter, because as the Custodian of the Two Holy Places and the King of Saudi Arabia, you hold a very high station in the Muslim *Ummah*. For located within your country are the two holiest sites in Islam— Makkah Al-Mukarramah and Madinah Al-Munawwarah—which to love constitutes a part of the faith of Muslims. These sites are also the centres of spiritual progress and are greatly revered by Muslims. In this light, all Muslims and Muslim governments confer special status upon you. This status requires that on the one hand, you should properly guide the Muslim *Ummah* and on the other, you should strive to create an atmosphere of peace and harmony within Muslim countries. You should also endeavour to develop mutual love and sympathy between Muslims and to enlighten them regarding the essence of:

رُحَمَاءُ بَيْنَهُمْ

Ultimately, you should strive to create peace in the entire world for the benefit of all of mankind. As Head of the Ahmadiyya Muslim Jama'at and the Khalifa of the Promised Messiah and Imam Mahdi (peace be upon him), it is my request that, irrespective of certain doctrinal disagreements that exist between the Ahmadiyya Muslim Jama'at and other sects of Islam, we should still unite in an effort to establish world peace. We should do our level best to educate the world regarding the true teachings of Islam, which are based on love and peace. By doing so, we can dispel the misconceptions in general that are embedded in the people of the West and the world about Islam. Enmity against other nations or groups should not hinder us from acting in a just manner. Allah the Almighty states in Verse 3 of *Surah Al-Ma'idah* of the Holy Qur'an:

وَلَا يَجْرِمَنَّكُمْ شَنَاٰنُ قَوْمٍ اَنْ صَدُّوْكُمْ عَنِ الْمَسْجِدِ الْحَرَامِ اَنْ

تَعْتَدُوْا ۘ وَتَعَاوَنُوْا عَلَى الْبِرِّ وَالتَّقْوٰى ۖ وَلَا تَعَاوَنُوْا عَلَى الْاِثْمِ وَالْعُدْوَانِ

$$وَاتَّقُوا اللّٰهَ ۚ اِنَّ اللّٰهَ شَدِيْدُ الْعِقَابِ ۞$$

'.... And let not the enmity of a people, that they hindered you from the Sacred Mosque, incite you to transgress. And help one another in righteousness and piety; but help not one another in sin and transgression. And fear Allah; surely, Allah is severe in punishment.'

This is the guiding principle that we should keep in view so that we can fulfil our duty to present the beautiful image of Islam to the world. It is with sentiments of heartfelt love and deep compassion for all Muslims worldwide that I am requesting you to play your role in this regard.

We find in the world today that some politicians and so-called scholars are planting seeds of hatred against Islam in an attempt to defame the Holy Prophet (peace and blessing of Allah be upon him). They try to present completely distorted interpretations of the teachings of the Holy Qur'an to achieve their aims. Further, the conflict between Palestine and Israel is worsening every day and hostilities between Israel and Iran have heightened to such an extent that their relationship has severely broken down. Such circumstances require that as an extremely important leader in the Muslim *Ummah* you should make every effort to resolve these disputes with justice and equality. The Ahmadiyya Muslim Jama'at does everything it possibly can to dispel the hatred against Islam, wherever and whenever it surfaces. Until the entire Muslim *Ummah* unites as one and makes efforts towards this, peace can never be established.

Thus, it is my request to you to do your utmost in this regard. If World War III is indeed destined to occur, at least we should strive to ensure that it does not originate from any Muslim country. No Muslim country or any Muslim individual anywhere in the world, today or in the future, will want to shoulder the blame for being the spark for a global catastrophe, the long-term effects of which will lead to future generations being born with defects or deformities, for if a World War breaks out now, it will surely be fought with nuclear weapons. We have already experienced just a glimpse of the utter devastation caused by atomic warfare when nuclear bombs were dropped on two cities in Japan during World War II.

Thus, O King of Saudi Arabia! Expend all your energy and influence to save the world from annihilation! May Allah the Almighty provide you with His Help and Succour, *Amin*. With prayers for you and for the entire Muslim *Ummah* of:

$$اِهْدِنَا الصِّرَاطَ الْمُسْتَقِيْمَ ۞$$

Wassalam,
Yours Sincerely,

MIRZA MASROOR AHMAD
Khalifatul Masih V
Head of the worldwide
Ahmadiyya Muslim Community

LETTER TO THE PREMIER OF THE STATE COUNCIL OF THE PEOPLE'S REPUBLIC OF CHINA

بِسۡمِ اللّٰهِ الرَّحۡمٰنِ الرَّحِيۡمِ

نَحۡمَدُهٗ وَنُصَلِّیۡ عَلٰی رَسُوۡلِهِ الۡکَرِیۡمِ

وعلٰی عبدِہِ المسیحِ الموعود

خدا کے فضل اور رحم کے ساتھ

ھوالناصر

MIRZA MASROOR AHMAD
HEAD OF THE AHMADIYYA COMMUNITY
IN ISLAM

16 Gressenhall Road
Southfields, London
SW18 5QL, UK

His Excellency,

Premier of the State Council of the People's Republic of China

Mr Wen Jiabao

Zhongnanhai, China

9 April 2012

Dear Premier,

I am sending this letter to you through one of our representatives of the Ahmadiyya Muslim Community. He is the President of our Community in Kababir, Israel and was invited by the Minister for Minorities in China. Our representative was introduced to Chinese officials during a visit by a delegation from China, which included the Deputy Minister for Minorities, to our Mission House in Kababir.

The Ahmadiyya Muslim Community is that sect in Islam which firmly believes that the Messiah and Reformer, who was destined to appear in this age as the Mahdi for the guidance of Muslims, as the Messiah for the guidance of Christians and as a guide for the reformation of all mankind, has indeed arrived in accordance with the prophecies of the Holy Prophet Muhammad (peace be upon him), and thus we have accepted him. His name was Hadhrat Mirza Ghulam Ahmad (peace be upon him) from Qadian, India. In accordance with God Almighty's command, he laid the foundation for the Ahmadiyya Muslim Community in 1889. By the time he passed away in 1908, hundreds of thousands of people had joined the fold of the Community. After his demise, the institution of Khilafat was established. Currently, we are in the era of the 5th Khilafat, and I am the 5th Khalifa of the Promised Messiah (peace be upon him).

An extremely important and fundamental aspect of our teaching is that in this era religious wars should come to an end. Further, we believe that anyone who desires to convey or spread any teaching should only do so in a spirit and atmosphere of love, compassion and brotherhood so that he can become the source of establishing peace, reconciliation and harmony. This important aspect, which is based on the true teachings of Islam, is being promoted and propagated by the Ahmadiyya Muslim Community all over the world. The Community is now spread over 200 countries of the world, and consists of millions of followers.

I wish to convey the following message to you: that the world is currently passing through a most harrowing and perilous period. Indeed, it would appear that we are rapidly drawing closer to a world war. You are the leader of a great superpower. In addition, an enormous proportion of the world's population live under your governance. You also possess the right to use the power to veto when required in the United Nations. Hence, in this context, it is my request to you to play your role to save the world from the destruction that looms before us. Irrespective of nationality, religion, caste or creed, we should strive to our utmost to save humanity.

In China, after the revolution took place, there was great progress and change. Honourable Mao Zedong, who was a great leader of your nation, established the foundation for high moral standards, which can also be described in other words as the most excellent standard of human values. Although you do not believe in the existence of God and your principles are based on morality, I would like to make it clear that our God, Who is the God as portrayed by Islam, revealed the Qur'an as guidance for all mankind, and the Qur'an inculcates all such morals that you act upon, but it is also filled with even further moral guidance. It contains beautiful teachings expounding the means of sustenance for humanity and establishing human values. If the world—the Muslim world in particular—adopt these Qur'anic teachings, all problems and conflicts will be resolved and an atmosphere of peace and harmony will be fostered.

Today, the Ahmadiyya Muslim Community endeavours to further this very purpose and objective in every part of the world. Through our peace symposiums and through numerous meetings that I hold with various categories of people and groups from all walks of life, I remind the world of this vital goal. It is my prayer that the leaders of the world act with wisdom and do not allow mutual enmities between nations and people on a small-scale to erupt into a global conflict. It is also my request to you that, as a great superpower of the world, play your role to establish world peace. Save the world from the horrifying consequences of a world war, for if such a war breaks out, it will come to an end with the use of atomic weapons. It is quite possible that as a result, parts of certain countries and areas of the world will be obliterated off the face of the earth. The effects and aftermath of an atomic war will not be limited to just the immediate devastation, rather, the long-term effects will result in future generations being born disabled or with defects. Thus, expend all your energy, capabilities and resources in the effort to save humanity from such dreadful consequences. It will ultimately be to the benefit of your nation to act upon this. It is my prayer that all countries of the world, large and small, come to understand this message.

With best wishes and prayers,

Yours Sincerely,

MIRZA MASROOR AHMAD

Khalifatul Masih V

Head of the worldwide

Ahmadiyya Muslim Community

LETTER TO THE PRIME MINISTER
OF THE UNITED KINGDOM

بِسْمِ اللّٰهِ الرَّحْمٰنِ الرَّحِيْمِ

نَحْمَدُهُ وَ نُصَلِّی عَلٰی رَسُوْلِهِ الْکَرِیْمِ

وعلٰی عبدِهِ المسیح الموعود

خدا کے فضل اور رحم کے ساتھ

هو الناصر

MIRZA MASROOR AHMAD
HEAD OF THE AHMADIYYA COMMUNITY
IN ISLAM

16 Gressenhall Road
Southfields, London
SW18 5QL, UK

Prime Minister of the United Kingdom of
Great Britain and Northern Ireland
Rt. Hon. David Cameron
10 Downing Street, London
SW1A 2AA
United Kingdom

15 April 2012

Dear Prime Minister,

In light of the perilous and precarious circumstances that the world is currently passing through, I felt it necessary to write to you. As the Prime Minister of the United Kingdom, you have the authority to make decisions that will affect the future of your country, and the world at large. Today, the world stands in dire need of peace because the sparks of war can be seen all around the world. Conflicts between countries on a small-scale are threatening to erupt into a global conflict. We observe that the situation of the world today is similar to the situation in 1932, both economically and politically. There are many other similarities and parallels, which when combined together, form the same image today that was witnessed just prior to the outbreak of the Second World War. If these sparks ever truly ignite, we will witness the terrifying scenario of a Third World War. With numerous countries, large and small, possessing nuclear weapons, such a war would undoubtedly involve atomic warfare. The weapons available today are so destructive that they could lead to generation after generation of children being born with severe genetic or physical defects. Japan is the one country to have experienced the abhorrent consequences of atomic warfare, when it was attacked by nuclear bombs during the Second World War, annihilating two of its cities. Yet the nuclear bombs that were used at that time and which caused widespread devastation, were much less powerful than the atomic weapons that are possessed by even certain small nations today. Therefore, it is the duty of the superpowers to sit down together to find a solution to save humanity from the brink of disaster.

What causes great fear is the knowledge that the nuclear weapons in smaller countries could end up in the hands of trigger-happy people who either do not have the ability, or who choose not to think about the consequences of their actions. If the major powers do not act with justice, do not eliminate the frustrations of smaller nations and do not adopt great and wise policies, then the situation will spiral out of all control and the destruction that will follow is beyond our comprehension and imagination. Even the majority of the world's population who do desire peace will also become engulfed by this devastation.

Thus, it is my ardent wish and prayer that you and the leaders of all major nations come to understand this dreadful reality, and so instead of adopting aggressive policies and utilising force to achieve your aims and objectives, you should strive to adopt policies that promote and secure justice.

If we look at the recent past, Britain ruled over many countries and left behind a high standard of justice and religious freedom, especially in the Sub-Continent of India and Pakistan. When the Founder of the Ahmadiyya Muslim Community congratulated Her Majesty, Queen Victoria, on her Diamond Jubilee and conveyed to her the message of Islam, he especially prayed for God to generously reward the British Government due to the manner in which it governed justly and with equity. He greatly praised the British Government for its just policies and for granting religious freedom. In today's world, the British Government no longer rules over the Sub-Continent, but still principles of freedom of religion are deeply entrenched in British society and its laws, through which every person is granted religious freedom and equal rights. This year the Diamond Jubilee of Her Majesty, Queen Elizabeth II, is being celebrated, which gives Britain an opportunity to demonstrate its standards of justice and honesty to the world. The history of the Ahmadiyya Muslim Community demonstrates that we have always acknowledged this justice whenever displayed by Britain and we hope that in future also, justice will remain a defining characteristic of the British Government, not only in religious matters, but in every respect that you will never forget the good qualities of your nation from the past and that in the current world situation, Britain will play its role in establishing peace worldwide.

It is my request that at every level and in every direction we must try our level best to extinguish the flames of hatred. Only if we are successful in this effort, will we be enabled to guarantee brighter futures for our generations to come. However, if we fail in this task, there should be no doubt in our minds that as result of nuclear warfare, our future generations everywhere will have to bear the horrific consequences of our actions and they will never forgive their elders for leading the world into a global catastrophe. I again remind you that Britain is also one of those countries that can and does exert influence in the developed world as well as in developing countries. You can guide this world, if you so desire, by fulfilling the requirements of equity and justice. Thus, Britain and other major powers should play their role towards establishing world peace. May God the Almighty enable you and other world leaders to understand this message.

With best wishes and with prayers,

Yours Sincerely,

MIRZA MASROOR AHMAD
Khalifatul Masih V
Head of the worldwide
Ahmadiyya Muslim Community

LETTER TO THE CHANCELLOR
OF GERMANY

بِسۡمِ اللّٰهِ الرَّحۡمٰنِ الرَّحِیۡمِ

نَحۡمَدُہٗ وَ نُصَلِّیۡ عَلٰی رَسُوۡلِهِ الۡکَرِیۡمِ

وعلٰی عبدہِ المسیح الموعود

خدا کے فضل اور رحم کے ساتھ

هوالناصــر

واجۡعَلۡ لَّنَا مِنۡ لَّدُنۡکَ سُلۡطٰنًا نَّصِیۡرًا

اِنَّا فَتَحۡنَا لَکَ فَتۡحًا مُّبِیۡنًا

اللّٰهُ یَبۡدَؤُا وَاللّٰه ...

MIRZA MASROOR AHMAD
HEAD OF THE AHMADIYYA COMMUNITY
IN ISLAM

16 Gressenhall Road
Southfields, London
SW18 5QL, UK

Her Excellency
Chancellor of Germany
Angela Merkel
Bundeskanzleramt
Willy-Brandt-Str.1
10557 Berlin

15 April 2012

Dear Chancellor,

In light of the alarming and extremely worrying state of affairs in the world today, I considered it necessary to write to you. As the Chancellor of Germany, a country which has significant power and influence in the world, you have the authority to make decisions that will affect your country and the entire world. Today, when the world is becoming divided into blocs, extremism is escalating and the financial, political and economic situation is worsening, there is an urgent need to extinguish all kinds of hatred and to lay the foundation for peace. This can only be achieved by respecting all of the sentiments of each and every person. However, as this is not being implemented properly, honestly and with virtue, the world situation is rapidly spiralling out of control. We observe that the requirements of justice are not being fulfilled by most nations, and as a result, the foundation for another World War has already been laid. Numerous countries, both large and small, now possess nuclear weapons. Thus, if a World War now breaks out, it is likely that it will not be fought with conventional weapons; rather, it will be fought with atomic weapons. The destruction that will result from a nuclear conflict will be utterly devastating. Its effects will not be limited to only the immediate aftermath; rather future generations will suffer from the long-term effects and will be born with serious medical and genetic defects.

Thus, it is my belief that to establish world peace, true justice is required, and the sentiments and the religious practices of all people should be honoured. I appreciate that many Western countries have generously permitted the people of poor or under-developed nations to settle in their respective countries, amongst whom are Muslims as well. Undoubtedly, there is a minority of so-called Muslims who act completely inappropriately and create distrust in the hearts of the people of the Western nations. However, it should be clear that their acts have no link with Islam whatsoever. Such extremists do not truly love the Holy Prophet Muhammad (peace be upon him), who brought a message of peace, love and reconciliation to the world. Indeed, the actions of just a handful of misguided people should not be used as a basis to raise objections against our religion and to hurt the sentiments of the majority of sincere and innocent Muslims. Peace in society is a two-way process and can only be established if all parties work together towards mutual reconciliation. Due to the mistrust in the hearts of the people in the West, instead of relationships between nations and people improving, the reaction of some non-Muslims is getting worse by the day and is creating a chasm between the Muslim and non-Muslim world.

We observe that on the basis of the misguided acts of certain Muslim groups and nations, the vested interests of some of the major powers are given preference to honesty and justice. Some of the powerful countries of the world desire to maintain easy access to the wealth and resources of certain countries and wish to avoid competing countries from having complete access to these same resources. That is why decisions are often made on the basis of helping people, or establishing world peace. Further, a major factor underlying the current political circumstances in the world is the economic downturn, which is pulling us towards another World War. If truth was truly being exhibited then some of these countries would derive benefit from each other in a just manner, by forming proper industrial and economic ties, based on fair dealings. They would not try to derive illegitimate benefit from the resources of one another, but instead would seek to come together and mutually assist one another. In short, the disorder prevalent in the world today is based upon one overriding factor, and that is a complete lack of justice, which is causing widespread anxiety and restlessness.

Thus, it is my request that strive to your utmost to prevent a World War from breaking out. Utilise all your energy, resources and influence to save the world from the horrific destruction that looms before us. According to reports, Germany will be providing three advanced submarines to Israel which could be armed with nuclear weapons. One German Professor has stated that such a decision will only serve to flare up the already heightened tensions between Israel and Iran. We must remember that nuclear weapons are not possessed by only the major powers of the world; rather, even relatively smaller countries now possess nuclear weapons. What is worrying is that in some of these small countries the leaders are trigger-happy, and appear unconcerned of the consequences of using such weapons. Therefore, once again, it is my humble request to you that try your level best to establish world peace. If we fail in this task there should be no doubt in our minds that a nuclear conflict will cause devastation that will lead to generation after generation being born with defects, and who will never forgive their elders for leading us into a global catastrophe. May God the Almighty enable you, and all world leaders, to understand this message.

With best wishes and with prayers,

Yours Sincerely,

MIRZA MASROOR AHMAD
Khalifatul Masih V
Head of the worldwide
Ahmadiyya Muslim Community

LETTER TO THE PRESIDENT OF
THE FRENCH REPUBLIC

بِسْمِ اللهِ الرَّحْمٰنِ الرَّحِيْمِ

نَحْمَدُهُ وَ نُصَلِّى عَلىٰ رَسُوْلِهِ الْكَرِيْمِ

وعلىٰ عبدہ المسیح الموعود

خدا کے فضل اور رحم کے ساتھ

هوالنَّاصِـــر

MIRZA MASROOR AHMAD
HEAD OF THE AHMADIYYA COMMUNITY
IN ISLAM

16 Gressenhall Road
Southfields, London
SW18 5QL, UK

President of the French Republic
His Excellency François Hollande
Palais de l'Elysee
55, Rue du Faubourg Saint-Honore
75008 Paris, France

16 May 2012

Dear Mr President,

I would like to first of all take this opportunity to congratulate you on being elected as the new President of France. This is certainly a vast responsibility that has been entrusted to you, and thus I hope and pray that the people of France, and indeed the entire world, come to benefit from your leadership. In light of the rapidly deteriorating state of affairs in the world, I recently wrote a letter to your predecessor, President Nicolas Sarkozy. In the letter I reminded President Sarkozy about his responsibilities as a world leader to uphold justice and I requested him to use all his power and influence to prevent a World War from breaking out. As the newly elected President of France, I considered it necessary to write to you also with the same message, because you now have the authority to make decisions that will affect your nation, and the world at large. It is my belief that the world's governments ought to be extremely concerned at the current circumstances in the world. Injustices and hostilities between nations are threatening to boil over into a global conflict. During the last century, two World Wars were fought. After the First World War, the League of Nations was established, however, the requirements of justice were not fulfilled and consequently, this led to the Second World War, culminating in the use of atom bombs. Subsequently, the United Nations was established for the protection of human rights and to maintain global peace. Thus, the means for avoiding wars were considered, yet today we observe that the foundation for a Third World War has already been laid. Numerous countries, both small and large, possess atom bombs. What is worrying is that some of the smaller nuclear powers are irresponsible and ignorant about the devastating consequences of such weapons. It is not inconceivable that if nuclear weapons are used, the horrific aftermath will become immediately manifest and that day will be like Doomsday. The weapons available today are so destructive that they could lead to generation after generation of children being born with severe genetic or physical defects. It is said that in Japan, the one country to have experienced the devastating destruction of atomic warfare, even though seven decades have passed, the effects of the atom bombs are still continuing to be manifest on newborn children.

Thus, it is my humble request that strive to your utmost to extinguish the enmities and mistrust between the Muslim and non-Muslim world. Some European countries hold significant reservations regarding the teachings and traditions of Islam and have placed certain restrictions on them, whilst others are considering how to do so. The animosity that some extremist so-called Muslims already hold towards the West might lead them to reacting in an inappropriate manner, which would lead to further religious intolerance and dissention. Islam, however, is a peace-loving religion, which does not teach us to do wrong to stop something wrong. We, the Ahmadiyya Muslim Community, follow this principle and believe in peaceful solutions to all matters.

Sadly, we find that a small minority of Muslims present a completely distorted image of Islam and act upon their misguided beliefs. I say out of love for the Holy Prophet Muhammad (peace be upon him), who was the '*Mercy for all Mankind*', that you should not believe this to be the real Islam and thus use such misguided acts as a licence to hurt the sentiments of the peaceful majority of Muslims. Recently, a merciless and heartless person shot dead some French soldiers in the South of France for no reason, and then some days later, he entered a school and killed three innocent Jewish children and one of their teachers. We also see such cruelties regularly come to pass in other Muslim countries and so all of these acts are giving the opponents of Islam fuel to vent their hatred and a basis upon which to pursue their goals on a large scale. As a Muslim, I shall make it absolutely clear that Islam does not permit cruelty or oppression in any way, shape or form. The Holy Qur'an has deemed the killing of one innocent person without reason akin to killing all mankind. This is an injunction that is absolute and without exception. The Qur'an further states that even if any country or people hold enmity towards you that must not stop you from acting in a fully just and fair manner when dealing with them. Enmities or rivalries should not lead you to taking revenge, or to acting disproportionately. If you desire conflicts to be resolved in the best manner, endeavour to search for amicable solutions. I appreciate that many Western countries have generously permitted the people of poor or under-developed nations to settle in their respective countries, amongst whom are Muslims as well. Indeed, many Muslims live in your country and thus are also your citizens. The majority are law-abiding and sincere. Moreover, Islam clearly states that love for one's country is part of the faith. The Ahmadiyya Muslim Community acts and promotes this message throughout the world. This is my message to you also, that if this true teaching of Islam is spread everywhere, then the requirements of showing love to one's nation and peace, will remain established within each country and between countries of the world.

My humble request to you, and indeed to all world leaders, is that instead of using force to suppress other nations, use diplomacy, dialogue and wisdom. The major powers of the world such as France, should play their role towards establishing peace. They should not use the acts of smaller countries as a basis to disturb world harmony. Thus, I again remind you to strive to your utmost to prevent the major and minor powers from erupting into a Third World War. There should be no doubt in our minds that if we fail in this task then the effects and aftermath of such a war will not be limited to only the poor countries of Asia, Europe and the Americas, rather, our future generations will have to bear the horrific consequences of our actions and children everywhere in the world will be born with defects. It is my prayer that the leaders of the world act with wisdom and do not allow mutual enmities between nations and people on a small-scale to erupt into a global conflict. May God the Exalted enable you, and all world leaders, to comprehend this message.

With best wishes and with prayers,
Yours Sincerely,

MIRZA MASROOR AHMAD
Khalifatul Masih V
Head of the worldwide Ahmadiyya Muslim Community

LETTER TO HER MAJESTY
THE QUEEN OF
THE UNITED KINGDOM AND
COMMONWEALTH REALMS

بِسْمِ اللهِ الرَّحْمٰنِ الرَّحِيْمِ

نَحْمَدُهُ وَ نُصَلِّیْ عَلیٰ رَسُوْلِهِ الْكَرِيْمِ

وعلیٰ عبدِهِ الْمَسِيْح الموعود

خدا کے فضل اور رحم کے ساتھ

هُوَالنَّاصِرُ

MIRZA MASROOR AHMAD
HEAD OF THE AHMADIYYA COMMUNITY
IN ISLAM

16 Gressenhall Road
Southfields, London
SW18 5QL, UK

Her Majesty, Queen Elizabeth II
Queen of the United Kingdom and Commonwealth Realms
Buckingham Palace
London SW1A 1AA
United Kingdom

19 April 2012

Your Majesty,

As Head of the Ahmadiyya Muslim Community, and on behalf of the millions of members of the Ahmadiyya Muslim Community worldwide, I express my heartfelt congratulations to Her Majesty, the Queen, on the joyous occasion of the Diamond Jubilee. We are exceptionally grateful to God Almighty for enabling us to partake in this glorious celebration. In particular, all Ahmadi Muslims who are citizens of the United Kingdom take great pleasure and pride in the occasion of the Diamond Jubilee. Therefore, on their behalf, I convey sincere and heartfelt congratulations to Her Majesty. May God the Exalted keep our generous Queen perpetually in happiness and contentment.

I beseech the Noble God, Who created the heavens and the earth and filled them with countless blessings for our sustenance, that may He always grant our Queen, whose generous rule comprises many sovereign states and commonwealth nations, with peace, tranquillity and security. Just as Her Majesty is loved and respected by all her subjects, old and young, it is our prayer that Her Majesty comes to be loved by the Angels of God. May the All-Powerful and Mighty God shower Her Majesty generously with His countless spiritual bounties and blessings, just as He has granted her with worldly blessings in abundance. Through these blessings, may all citizens of this great nation be enabled to recognise the Supreme Lord and come to live in mutual love and affection. Irrespective of colour, creed, nationality or religion may all citizens of the United Kingdom show respect and honour to one another, to such a degree, that the positive impact and influence of this attitude extends beyond these shores and spreads to the people of other countries of the world also. May the world, much of which today is embroiled in wars, disorder and enmities instead become a haven of peace, love, brotherhood and friendship. It is my strong belief that the vision and efforts of Her Majesty can play a prominent role towards achieving this critical and overarching objective.

In the last century, two World Wars were fought in which millions of lives were lost. If today grievances between nations continue to increase, it will ultimately lead to the outbreak of another World War. The likely use of nuclear weapons in a World War will mean that the world will witness untold and horrifying destruction. May God prevent such a catastrophe from occurring and may all people of the world adopt wisdom and sense. It is my humble request to Her Majesty to use the joyous celebration of the Diamond Jubilee, as a favour to mankind, to remind all people that all nations, whether large or small, should come to live in mutual love, peace and harmony.

In this context, on the auspicious occasion of the Diamond Jubilee, I would also humbly request Her Majesty to give the world the message that the followers of any religion, and even those who do not believe in God, should always respect the sentiments of the people of any other faith. Today, misconceptions regarding Islam are prevalent in the world. This on the one hand wounds the sentiments of peace-loving Muslims, whilst on the other, develops contempt and mistrust against Islam in the hearts of non-Muslims. Thus, it will be an act of great kindness and a favour to the followers of all religions, and indeed the entire world, if Her Majesty counsels all people to be respectful to religions and their followers. May the Noble Lord provide His Help and Succour to our Queen in the fulfilment of this objective.

As I mentioned at the beginning of this letter, I am the Head of the worldwide Ahmadiyya Muslim Community. In this regard, I would like to provide a very brief overview of our Community. The Ahmadiyya Muslim Community firmly believes that the Promised Messiah and Reformer who, according to the prophecies of the Holy Prophet Muhammad (peace be upon him) and past Prophets was destined to appear in this age, is none other than Hadhrat Mirza Ghulam Ahmad of Qadian (peace be upon him). In 1889, he founded a pure and righteous community—the Ahmadiyya Muslim Community. His purpose for forming this Community was to establish a relationship between man and God and to incline people towards fulfilling the rights of one another so that they can live in mutual respect, and in goodwill. When Hadhrat Mirza Ghulam Ahmad (peace be upon him) passed away in 1908, he had approximately 400,000 followers. After his demise, the system of Khilafat was established in accordance with the Divine Will and currently, this humble servant of God is the Fifth Khalifa of the Promised Messiah (peace be upon him). Thus, the Ahmadiyya Muslim Community endeavours to further the mission of its Founder throughout the world. Our message is one of love, reconciliation and brotherhood and our motto is *'Love for All, Hatred for None'*. Indeed, this embodies the beautiful teachings of Islam in a nutshell.

It would be pertinent to mention here that it is a pleasant coincidence that during the era of the Founder of the Ahmadiyya Muslim Community, the Diamond Jubilee of Her Majesty, Queen Victoria, was celebrated. At the time, the Founder of the Ahmadiyya Community wrote a book, called *A Gift for the Queen*, in which he wrote a message of congratulations to Queen Victoria. In his message, Hadhrat Mirza Ghulam Ahmad (peace be upon him) congratulated the Queen on her Diamond Jubilee, and for the manner in which all subjects under her rule, including the people of the Sub-Continent of India, were provided with justice and religious freedom and lived in peace. He presented the beautiful teachings of Islam and elucidated the purpose of his advent and claim. Although the people of the Sub-Continent have now been granted independence by the British Government, the fact that in Britain the Government has allowed people of diverse backgrounds and religions to live here, and has granted them all equal rights, freedom of religion and freedom to express and to propagate their beliefs, is ample proof of Britain's very high levels of tolerance.

Today, there are thousands of Ahmadi Muslims living in the United Kingdom. Many of them have fled here to seek refuge from the persecution they faced in their own countries. Under the generous rule of Her Majesty, they enjoy a peaceful life in which they receive justice, and freedom of religion. For this generosity, I would like to once again express my gratitude from my heart to our noble Queen.

I shall conclude my letter with the following prayer for Her Majesty, which is virtually the same prayer that was offered by the Founder of the Ahmadiyya Muslim Community for Her Majesty, Queen Victoria:

"O Powerful and Noble God! Through your Grace and Blessings keep our honoured Queen forever joyful, in the same way that we are living joyfully under her benevolent and benign rule. Almighty God! Be kind and loving to her, in the same way that we are living in peace and prosperity under her generous and kind rule."

Further, it is my prayer that may God the Exalted guide our honoured Queen in a manner that pleases Him. May God the Almighty also guide the progeny of Her Majesty to become established on the Truth and to guiding others towards it. May the attributes of justice and freedom continue to remain the guiding principles of the British Monarchy. I once again congratulate Her Majesty from my heart on this occasion of great joy. I present my heartfelt and sincere congratulations to our noble Queen.

With best wishes and with prayers,
Yours Sincerely,

MIRZA MASROOR AHMAD
Khalifatul Masih V
Head of the worldwide
Ahmadiyya Muslim Community

LETTER TO THE SUPREME LEADER OF THE ISLAMIC REPUBLIC OF IRAN

MIRZA MASROOR AHMAD
HEAD OF THE AHMADIYYA COMMUNITY
IN ISLAM

بِسْمِ اللّٰهِ الرَّحْمٰنِ الرَّحِيْمِ

نَحْمَدُهٗ وَ نُصَلِّیْ عَلٰی رَسُوْلِهِ الْكَرِیْمِ

وعلٰی عبدِهِ المسیح الموعود

خدا کے فضل اور رحم کے ساتھ

ہوالناصر

16 Gressenhall Road
Southfields, London
SW18 5QL, UK

Supreme Leader of the Islamic Republic of Iran
Ayatollah Syed Ali Hosseini Khamenei
Tehran, Iran

14 May 2012

Respected Ayatollah,

Assalamo Alaikum Wa Rahmatullahe Wa Barakatohu,

Allah the Almighty has enabled you to serve Islam in Iran and presently, the Government of Iran also functions under your auspices. This requires that we strive to our utmost to convey the correct Islamic teachings to the world. As Muslims, we should endeavour to teach the world to live in peace, love and harmony. In particular, Muslim leaders need to urgently pay heed to this. For this reason, it is my request to you to draw the attention of your Government towards its responsibilities to establishing peace in the world. If Iran is attacked it has the right to defend itself to save the country, however it should not instigate aggression and take the first step forward into any conflict. Instead, an effort should be made to leave aside religious differences and to try and unite upon common values. It is this very approach that we find was adopted in the history of Islam.

I am writing this letter to you for the reason that I am a believer, Successor and the Khalifa of the Promised Messiah and Imam Mahdi (peace be upon him), whose advent in this age was prophesied by the Holy Prophet Muhammad (peace be upon him). The Community he established is known as the Ahmadiyya Muslim Community. With the Grace of Allah, the Community has now spread to 200 countries of the world and has millions of devoted followers across the globe. It is our ardent desire to guide the world towards living in mutual love and peace. To this end, I constantly draw the attention of people from all walks of life. Hence, I recently wrote to the Prime Minister of Israel, the President of the United States of America and also other world leaders. I have also written to Pope Benedict XVI in this regard.

As the spiritual leader of a large Islamic nation, I hope that you will come to agree that if the entire Muslim *Ummah* unites and works together, world peace can be established. We should not pointlessly add fuel to enmities and grudges, rather, we should search for opportunities to establish peace and tranquillity. Further, even enmity or opposition against others should not be devoid of justice. This is what we have been taught in the Holy Qur'an:

'O ye who believe! be steadfast in the cause of Allah, bearing witness in equity; and let not a people's enmity incite you to act otherwise than with justice. Be always just, that is nearer to righteousness. And fear Allah. Surely, Allah is aware of what you do.' (*Surah Al-Ma'idah*, Verse 9).

May Allah enable the entire Muslim *Ummah* and all Muslim governments to understand my message so that they prepare themselves to play their respective roles in an effort to establish peace in the world.

It is my love for mankind, developed out of a love for the entire Muslim *Ummah*, and also because of being a member of the *Ummah* of the *'Mercy for all mankind'* myself, that has led me to writing this letter. May Allah enable the leaders of the world to understand my words and may they actively play a role in establishing world peace. Otherwise, if the haste and recklessness of any nation leads to a full blown war between two nations, such a conflict will not be limited to only those countries; rather the flames of war will engulf the entire world. Thus, it is entirely plausible that a World War will break out, which will not be fought with conventional weapons, but rather with atomic weapons. A nuclear war will result in such horrific and devastating consequences that its aftermath will not only affect those present in the world at the time, rather the long-term effects of such a war would provide the terrifying 'gift' to future generations of being born with disabilities and defects. For this reason, no country should assume they are safe from the impending destruction.

Therefore, once again, in the name of Allah and His Messenger and out of compassion and love for humanity, I request you to play your role in establishing peace in the world.

With best wishes and with prayers,

Wassalam,
Yours Sincerely,

MIRZA MASROOR AHMAD
Khalifatul Masih V
Head of the worldwide
Ahmadiyya Muslim Community

LETTER TO THE PRESIDENT OF THE RUSSIAN FEDERATION

MIRZA MASROOR AHMAD
HEAD OF THE AHMADIYYA COMMUNITY
IN ISLAM

بِسْمِ اللهِ الرَّحْمٰنِ الرَّحِيْمِ

نَحْمَدُهُ وَ نُصَلِّى عَلٰى رَسُوْلِهِ الْكَرِيْمِ

وعلٰى عبدِهِ المسيح الموعود

خدا کے فضل اور رحم کے ساتھ

هو الناصر

16 Gressenhall Road
Southfields, London
SW18 5QL, UK

His Excellency
Mr. Vladimir Putin
President of the Russian Federation
The Kremlin
23, Ilyinka Street,
Moscow 103132 Russia

18 September 2013

Dear Mr President,

I am writing this letter to you as the Head of the Ahmadiyya Muslim Community, an entirely peace-loving and peace-promoting community spread across 204 countries of the world.

Due to the prevailing circumstances in the world, I have been reminding the people of the world in my different discourses and addresses, their duty and responsibilities towards their Creator and their fellow beings. Regrettably, I did not have the chance to speak to you directly, however the present day escalating situation in Syria has prompted me to write to you and commend your effort in bringing the world together onto a table of dialogue rather than the battlefield. An attack would risk a war not only in the region but could have led to a world war. I was therefore very pleased to read your recent article in a major Western newspaper in which you highlighted that such a course of action was extremely dangerous and could lead to the war spreading. Due to your stand, the major powers have refrained and have adopted a more conciliatory stance, agreeing to resolve this issue through diplomatic channels. Certainly, I believe that this has saved the world from a colossal and huge destruction. I particularly agreed with your point that if countries decided to act independently and made unilateral decisions then the United Nations would suffer the same fate as the League of Nations and would fail. Certainly, the sparks of war recently ignited but thankfully they now seem to have subsided somewhat. May God the Almighty enable the risk of war to be eliminated altogether as a result of the positive step that has been taken. May the major powers come to care and respect the smaller nations and fulfil their due rights, rather than only being concerned for their own powers of veto.

In any case, your efforts towards establishing peace have obliged me to write this letter of thanks to you. I pray that this is not a temporary effort, but rather I hope and pray that you always make efforts towards peace. May Allah enable you to achieve this.

For the sake of world peace, wherever I have the opportunity, I draw the attention of people towards establishing peace through justice. Some of my addresses have been published in a book entitled, *World Crisis and Pathway to Peace*. I am enclosing a copy of this book as a gift for you.

With best wishes and with prayers,

MIRZA MASROOR AHMAD
Khalifatul Masih V
Head of the worldwide
Ahmadiyya Muslim Community

PUBLISHERS' NOTE

Please note that, in the translation that follows, words given in parentheses ( ) are the words of the Promised Messiah[as]. If any explanatory words or phrases are added by the translator for the purpose of clarification, they are put in square brackets [ ]. Footnotes given by the publishers are marked '[Publishers]'. All references, unless otherwise specified, are from the English translation of the Holy Qur'an by Ḥaḍrat Maulavī Sher Ali[ra].

The following abbreviations have been used. Readers are urged to recite the full salutations when reading the book:

sa *ṣallallāhu 'alaihi wa sallam*, meaning 'may peace and blessings of Allah be upon him,' is written after the name of the Holy Prophet Muhammad[sa].

as *'alaihis-salām*, meaning 'may peace be on him,' is written after the name of Prophets other than the Holy Prophet Muhammad[sa].

ra *raḍiyallāhu 'anhu/'anhā/'anhum*, meaning 'may Allah be pleased with him/her/them,' is written after the names of the Companions of the Holy Prophet Muhammad[sa] or of the Promised Messiah[as].

aba *ayyadahullāhu Ta'ālā binaṣrihil-'Azīz*, meaning 'may Allah the Almighty help him with his powerful support,' is written after the name of the present Head of the Aḥmadiyya Muslim Jamā'at, Ḥaḍrat Mirza Masroor Ahmad, Khalīfatul-Masīḥ V[aba].

In transliterating Arabic words we have adopted the following system established by the Royal Asiatic Society.

ا   at the beginning of a word, pronounced as *a, i, u* preceded by a very slight aspiration, like *h* in the English word *honour*.

ث   *th*, pronounced like *th* in the English word *thing*.

ح   *ḥ*, a guttural aspirate, stronger than *h*.

خ   *kh*, pronounced like the Scotch *ch* in *loch*.

ذ   *dh*, pronounced like the English *th* in *that*.

ص   *ṣ*, strongly articulated *s*.

ض   *ḍ*, similar to the English *th* in *this*.

ط   *ṭ*, strongly articulated palatal *t*.

ظ   *ẓ*, strongly articulated *z*.

ع   ', a strong guttural, the pronunciation of which must be learnt by the ear

غ   *gh*, a sound approached very nearly in the *r grasseye* in French, and in the German *r*. It requires the muscles of the throat to be in the 'gargling' position whilst pronouncing it.

ق   *q*, a deep guttural *k* sound.

ء   ', a sort of catch in the voice.

Short vowels are represented by:

a   for ——— (like *u* in *bud*)

i   for ——— (like *i* in *bid*)

u   for ——— (like *oo* in *wood*)

Long vowels by:

ā   for ——— or ‏ا‎ (like *a* in *father*);

ī   for ‏ى‎ ——— or ——— (like *ee* in *deep*);

ū   for ‏و‎ ——— (like *oo* in *root*);

Other:

ai   for ‏ى‎ ——— (like *i* in *site*);

au   for ‏و‎ ——— (resembling *ou* in *sound*)

The consonants not included in the above list have the same phonetic value as in the principal languages of Europe. While the Arabic ‏ن‎ is represented by *n*, we have indicated the Urdu ‏ن‎ as *ń*. Curved commas are used in the system of transliteration, ' for ‏ع‎, ' for ‏ء‎.

We have not transliterated Arabic words which have become part of English language, e.g. Islam, Qur'an, Hadith, Mahdi, jihad, Ramadan and ummah. The Royal Asiatic Society rules of transliteration for names of persons, places and other terms, could not be followed throughout the book as many of the names contain non-Arabic characters and carry a local transliteration and pronunciation style which in itself is also not consistent either.

The Publishers

GLOSSARY

Ahmadiyya Muslim Jamā'at—The Community of Muslims who have accepted the claims of Ḥaḍrat Mirza Ghulam Ahmad[as] of Qadian as the Promised Messiah and Mahdi. The Community was established by Ḥaḍrat Mirza Ghulam Ahmad[as] in 1889, and is now under the leadership of his fifth *khalīfah*—Ḥaḍrat Mirza Masroor Ahmad (may Allah be his help). The Community is also known as **Jamā'at-e-Ahmadiyya**. A member of the Community is called an **Aḥmadī Muslim** or simply an **Aḥmadī**.

Al-Imam al-Mahdi—The title given to the Promised Reformer by the Holy Prophet Muhammad[sa]; it means the guided leader.

Āmīn—A term said after a prayer meaning, 'May Allah make it so.'

Assalāmo 'alaikum wa raḥmatullāhe wa barakātohū—Traditional Islamic greeting, meaning, may peace be on you, and the mercy of Allah and His grace.

Ḥaḍrat—A term of respect used for a person of established righteousness and piety; lit. 'His/Her Holiness.'

Holy Prophet[sa]—A term used exclusively for the Founder of Islam, Ḥaḍrat Muhammad, may peace and blessings of Allah be upon him.

Holy Qur'an—The Book sent by Allah for the guidance of mankind. It was revealed word by word to the Holy Prophet Muhammad[sa] over a period of twenty-three years.

Khalīfah—Successor. A Khalīfah of Allah is a term used for a Prophet. Khalīfah of a Prophet refers to his Successor who continues his mission.

Khalīfatul-Masīḥ—A term used by the Aḥmadiyya Muslim Jamā'at to denote the Successors of the Promised Messiah[as].

Khilāfat—The literal meaning of the term is successorship.

Mahdi—The literal translation of this word is 'the guided one'. This is the title given by the Holy Prophet Muhammad[sa] to the awaited Reformer of the Latter Days.

The Promised Messiah—This term refers to the Founder of the Aḥmadiyya Muslim Jamā'at, Ḥaḍrat Mirza Ghulam Ahmad[as] of Qadian. He claimed that he had been sent by Allah in accordance with the prophecies of the Holy Prophet[sa] about the coming of *al-Imam al-Mahdi* (the Guided Leader) and Messiah.